THROUGHPUT ACCOUNTING

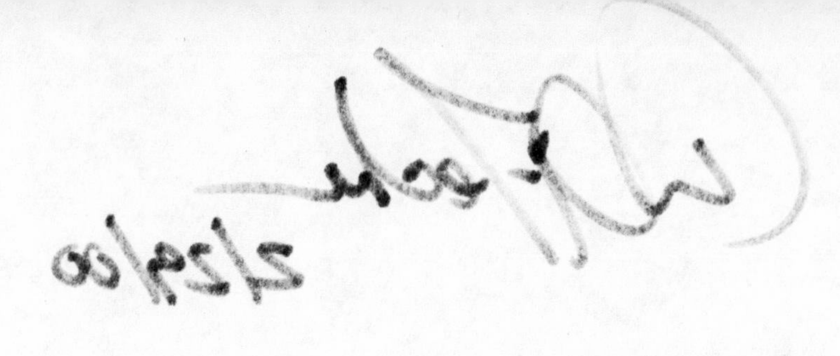

THROUGHPUT ACCOUNTING

TOC's Management Accounting System

Thomas Corbett

THE NORTH RIVER PRESS

Additional copies of this book can be obtained from your local bookstore or the publisher:

The North River Press
Publishing Corporation
P.O. Box 567
Great Barrington, MA 01230
(800) 486-2665 or (413) 528-0034

www.northriverpress.com

Manufactured in the United States of America

ISBN: 0-88427-158-7

To my grandfather, Favorino

Acknowledgements

I wish to thank CAPES and CNPq for the scholarships they granted me during my masters studies. I would also like to thank the Avraham Y. Goldratt Institute for giving me access to all of its studies on the Theory of Constraints, without which I would not have been able to finish this book.

I thank Antonio Augusto N. V. S. Pereira, Jun Aoki, Mário Alberto Machado and Murilo Fernandes Gabrielli, the professors on my masters examination board; Prof. Jacob Ancelevicz, Prof. Peter Kevin Spink and Prof. João Mário Csillag; my students; and the comments made by the readers of the first version of this book[1] for their criticism and contributions.

Without the collaboration of the companies where I helped to implement the Theory of Constraints (TOC), I would not have been able to include practical issues of Throughput Accounting in this book. In addition, I would like to especially thank Celso Calia and Evaldo Albuquerque for our numerous discussions and exchanges of ideas about management accounting.

[1] In Portuguese: *Contabilidade de Ganhos. A nova contabilidade gerencial de acordo com a teoria das restrições.* São Paulo: Nobel, 1997.

Contents

Introduction 1
1. The Role of Management Accounting 5
2. Cost Accounting's Obsolescence 11
3. Theory of Constraints (TOC) 23
4. Throughput Accounting Statements 41
5. Throughput Accounting v. Cost Accounting 81
6. The Damages Caused by Local Optimizations 93
7. Criticisms of Throughput Accounting 111
8. Other Decisions Using TOC 119
9. Paradigm Shift in Management Accounting 138
10. Cost World v. Throughput World 145
11. Conclusion 157
Bibliography 163
Appendix—Balanced Capacity 169

THROUGHPUT ACCOUNTING

Introduction

This book has two main objectives: 1) to outline a new approach to management accounting, based on the Theory of Constraints (TOC); and 2) to compare TOC's paradigm with the paradigm of traditional management, and in so doing demonstrate a possible alternative to the problems of modern management. I want to show the logic and simplicity behind TOC and hope that by doing so, you will be able to draw your own conclusions about how we should measure certain things in an organization.

I did not intend to write a complete treatment of management accounting or TOC. Often I make only a minor reference or offer a limited demonstration of a concept, and this may cause some confusion. To avoid any potential misunderstanding I provide more study material to those people interested in specific topics, I have included references whenever possible to books or articles where the reader can delve deeper into the concept being discussed.

This is not a book about strategies. Rather it is a book about how to make decisions according to the system's objectives. What I demonstrate here is a management information system that will enable managers to quickly see if their decisions increase their companies' profitability or not. A good information system is not a guarantee of success, but it certainly plays a fundamental part in the implementation of successful strategies.

TOC is far more comprehensive than what I will discuss here. It is a new paradigm for business created by the Israeli physicist, Dr. Eliyahu Goldratt. Many people think that TOC is simply another production administration methodology. This is due to the fact that the business novel entitled *The Goal* is the main promoter of the theory. In his book Goldratt demonstrates the principles of his theory using a manufacturing environment. Goldratt expanded his theory beyond production logistics in his 1994 business novel *It's Not Luck.*

In this book I will show a new decision-making methodology for business environments, specifically for industries, called Throughput Accounting (TA). I first read about these concepts in *The Goal,* and I studied them further by reading *The Haystack Syndrome.* At that time I was studying for my masters in Business Administration, with a major in management accounting, and these Goldratt books aroused my curiosity. After reading them I decided that I would write my thesis about TOC. As I was studying management accounting, I decided that I would compare TOC's methodology for management accounting with Activity-Based Costing (ABC), which is considered to be the correct option for a management accounting system. This book was born from that study and from the lack of such a book for the general public. But, fear not, I have changed many aspects of my original study to make for more pleasant reading. In particular I have tried to eliminate all the "academicisms" and have added some practical examples.

One of the greatest merits of this work is to bring together the ideas about Throughput Accounting in one book. The vast majority of this book's content comes from Eli Goldratt's ideas, books, articles and presentations. Nevertheless, Goldratt is not responsible for what I have written, or for my interpretation of his ideas. Other parts of this book come from discussions with other people, some of them TOC devotees, others cost accounting devotees, from the reading of other authors, from the implementations of this methodology in some companies and from discussions with my students.

The first chapter discusses the market situation and the role of management accounting in this context. The second chapter demonstrates some of cost accounting's flaws and also shows the rationale behind the development of cost accounting at the beginning of this century.

The third chapter reveals TOC's basic principles and its three performance measurements. In the fourth chapter I provide more detail about Throughput Accounting statements, and use some examples to show how to make decisions using these statements.

In the fifth chapter I compare the new paradigm of TOC-based throughput accounting with more conventional cost accounting methodologies, using Activity-Based Costing, presently the most accepted methodology. The choice of the cost accounting methodology to be compared with TOC is not that important, as all of them are based on the same basic assumptions (as we will see in chapter 9).

In the sixth chapter I reveal the assumptions behind cost accounting, and evaluate the consequences of using this paradigm. In the seventh chapter I discuss some of the criticism of Throughput Accounting.

In chapter 8 we will see how to make some other decisions using TOC (some decisions that we did not see in chapter 4). In the ninth chapter I will talk about paradigm shifts in management accounting.

The tenth chapter is a comparison between the strategies encouraged by cost accounting and the strategies suggested by TOC. The eleventh chapter is the conclusion.

I believe TOC is one of the main building blocks for a better paradigm to manage organizations. Currently the leading paradigm is scientific management. But TOC, together with other theories, has been challenging the status quo. Many people and organizations are trying to make contributions to a paradigm shift, but this is not easy; it requires a real revolution. Scientific management, already entrenched in our behavior and in our culture, makes the task even harder. However I do not want you to think that I believe scientific management is bad. Although I believe that it is one of the main causes for the extraordinary growth that industry has experienced this century, its time has passed. Right now we need other management methods that this paradigm cannot offer.

I hope this book will contribute to this paradigm shift by showing a new management tool for managerial accounting, and also by showing an alternative path for other management practices.

I believe that Goldratt will be a major contributor to the management principles of the next century. Goldratt brought concepts from physics to the business world and he is revolutionizing our way of managing and thinking. TOC's Thought Processes might provide the missing tools that will enable us to build what Peter Senge, author of *The Fifth Discipline*, called "The Learning Organization", an organization where change is the norm.

1
The Role of Management Accounting

1.1. Setting the Stage

Since the beginning of the century our society and organizations have changed greatly, and the business environment continues to change more all the time.

But types of accounting methods have not kept pace. The old cost accounting, for example, is:

- Too complicated, so few understand it.
- Unable to identify the products that most contribute to the company's profits, thus fail to help firms prosper.

By contrast, there is a move for a new form of accounting, known as Throughput Accounting (TA). It:

- Is simple.
- Is easily understood.
- Identifies products that most contribute to the profit picture, thus allowing managers to make good decisions fast.

In today's world, competition is fiercer than ever, demanding that companies adapt quickly. Companies have to make change a norm. One change is not enough. This point was popularized by the quality movements, by what they call "continuous improvement". Organizations have to be prepared for this new challenge, which involves, first of all, a change in mentality. Increasingly, success has a short life span and any advantage gained can be lost in a very short time. Organizations, as well as people, have to learn how to deal with this new change.

The problem lies in this new change. We get so attached to certain principles that we cannot see that things are changing, and we end up thinking we do not need to change the way we do things. However, not everyone is standing still. Within a constantly changing environment many organizations are also changing. They are trying to follow the changes and trying to find new ways of competing, and by doing so they are contributing to the market's dynamics. Most managers agree that focusing on the client is the best path for success, and it is with this vision in mind that new forms of organization are emerging, new forms that look for more flexibility and a better understanding of the market. This demands that everyone in the organization participate and understand what the organization does and where it wants to go, making us view the organization as a whole. With the objective of satisfying the consumer, real revolutions are taking place. Many assumptions that before were considered sacred cows, are now being questioned.

Many people talk about the need to change management, in order to make change a reality. Drucker talks a lot about change in management practices. Author W. Edwards Deming talks about the Profound Knowledge that we should absorb to be able to better manage our organizations. Senge, in his book *The Fifth Discipline,* also emphasizes learning, saying that we should question our view of reality.

These and other people advocate a significant change in management. We need to change our understanding of organizations and how we should manage them. The messages of the majority of the business gurus derive from a shared view of the organization; they are pointing in the same direction. They all advocate a systemic view of the organization; they instruct us to perceive the company as an organism in which all of the parts need to work in conjunction so that we can all contribute to the desired objective. They all agree that our conventional management models are obsolete.

In order to achieve this paradigm shift, we must abandon traditional management concepts and use new ones. This, in my view, is Goldratt's great contribution. Goldratt, like many other people, also talks about the need to change management, the need to view the company as a system, the need to make the company a learning organization, but he gives us the tools that might enable us to achieve that revolution. These tools are Goldratt's Thought Processes.

The Thought Processes are the basis for a learning organization, for creating an organization that causes change and, consequently, one that enters in a process of ongoing improvements.

Although all the business gurus are constantly advocating a radical change in management and the majority of us agree that it is necessary, very few companies are really changing. The great majority of them are still using management techniques developed nearly 100 years ago. Why?

The organizations that have not changed are caught in a conflict. On the one hand they perceive that to guarantee their profitability and their survival, they must not run any risks. They must have security, that is, protect themselves from fads, and in order to achieve this balance they must continue using the same management principles. What many of them do is improve the management principles they already use. On the other hand, to guarantee profitability and survival, they must adapt to the new reality, and for that to occur they have to change the way they manage. Therefore, in order to guarantee profitability and the survival of the company:

- Do not run risks
- Be sure to adapt to the new reality

In the eyes of these companies, to have security it is essential not to change and at the same time in order to adapt to the new reality, change is essential. Herein lies the conflict.

I hope this book will help some companies/people to get out of this conflict, showing that TOC adapts to the new reality and at the same time does not expose the organization to risks. The companies that are capable of escaping this conflict will have the greatest opportunities to achieve significant competitive advantages. In fact, and I hope this will be clear to you when you finish reading this book, the companies that do not change are the ones that run the greatest risks.

Moreover, many believe that their lack of competitiveness stems from causes out of their control: high taxes, unlawful competition from imported products, market instability, high interest rates, lack of qualified manpower, and so on. For many, an increase in their company's performance is dependent exclusively on the effort and goodwill of other people. I hope to show here that managers still have plenty of room to significantly improve their company's performance without depending on anyone, except themselves.

1.2. Management Accounting

All changes in the business environment have an impact on managerial accounting. This impact becomes evident when we analyze the severe criticism to which managerial accounting has been subjected.

> The explosion in technology is changing the basis of competition throughout the world. In order to compete effectively, companies must strive to manufacture sophisticated products at a low cost while maintaining high quality and providing outstanding customer service (short lead times). . . . A particularly important but not well understood difficulty is the role played by today's cost accounting systems. Information is not being provided in a format to help management identify, prioritize, and solve problems. Manufacturing managers are being asked to make important decisions *in spite of* available cost accounting information, not *because* it is relevant.[2]

Criticism is based on changes in the environment, changes that did not have a counterpart in management accounting. Unfortunately, management accounting's structure is still the same as it was at the beginning of the century.

The market (and therefore the companies) changed a lot since the beginning of the century, but management accounting did not. This stagnation made management accounting's information irrelevant; it is not fulfilling its goal anymore.

1.2.1. Management Accounting's Objective

Any organization needs an information system that guides and motivates managers to move towards the company's goal. They need to know in what direction to direct their efforts, to move the organization closer to its goal.

We can use a compass as an analogy for management accounting. The compass shows us the direction we are going, and we can then check to see if we are on the right course or if we need to make

[2] BERLINER and BRIMSON. *Cost Management for Today's Advanced Manufacturing.* Boston: Harvard Business School Press, 1988, p. 19.

any course corrections. If we are not on the right course, it gives us the right one.

The goal of a system must be determined by the owners of the system. In the case of industries, let us suppose that the goal is to make money now and in the future. The performance measurements used to verify whether the company is moving towards its goal are *Net Profit* (NP) and *Return On Investment* (ROI). These two measurements give the position of the company in relation to its goal, but they are not very useful for making day-to-day decisions. For the managers' day-to-day decisions it is necessary to have a bridge between their decisions/actions and the profitability of the company.

Management accounting has to make this connection, so that the managers can know what course to take. When measuring correctly the impact of local decisions on the global performance, management accounting also serves as a motivating factor, because it rewards those who positively contribute to the company's goal. Management accounting's goal is to provide managers with the information they need to make decisions in relation to the system's goal.

1.2.2. Relevance Lost

Nowadays management accounting is losing credibility. Even though there were many changes in the environment, it has not changed much since the beginning of the century. This has made the information supplied by management accounting useless. With the environment in constant change, companies cannot have distorted information. If your managerial accounting has not adapted to the new environment, you will not be able to compete. A good management accounting system is not the recipe for success, but it is a prerequisite for a company to be successful.

> An excellent management accounting system will not by itself guarantee success in today's environment... But an ineffective management accounting system can undermine superior product development, process improvement, and marketing efforts. Where an ineffective management accounting system prevails, the best outcome occurs when managers understand the irrelevance of the system and by-pass it by developing personalized information systems.[3]

[3] JOHNSON, H. Thomas and KAPLAN, Robert S. *Relevance Lost, the Rise and Fall of Management Accounting*. Boston: Harvard Business School Press, 1991, p. 4.

Management accounting cannot ignore the changes; it needs to evolve, to adapt to the new times.

There are a number of different proposed management accounting methodologies that try to correct this loss in relevance. Here I will deal with the methodology proposed by TOC, which I consider the best one, the one that is most in line with the new vision of the company, and I will compare it with the prevailing paradigm of management accounting, that is, cost accounting.

2
Cost Accounting's Obsolescence

Many people believe that the reasons for a company's lack of competitiveness are out of the control of its managers. Generally, they blame the government, the competitors, the globalization, the clients, the suppliers. To see if this reasoning is correct, that is, if the causes for lack of competitiveness are out of the control of their managers, let us analyze a situation where we do not have all these external causes.

Let us use a very simple example where all the external causes have been eliminated. Taxes are low, competition is not fierce, the market is constant and clients do not change their minds, employees are well trained, resources are new and the process is well controlled, suppliers are reliable, and interest rates are low. The only thing we need to define is the company's policies.

2.1. An Example

We are going to analyze a very simple company. It has two machines—one that cuts fabric and another one that sews the pieces together, making different kinds of shirts.

Figure 2-1

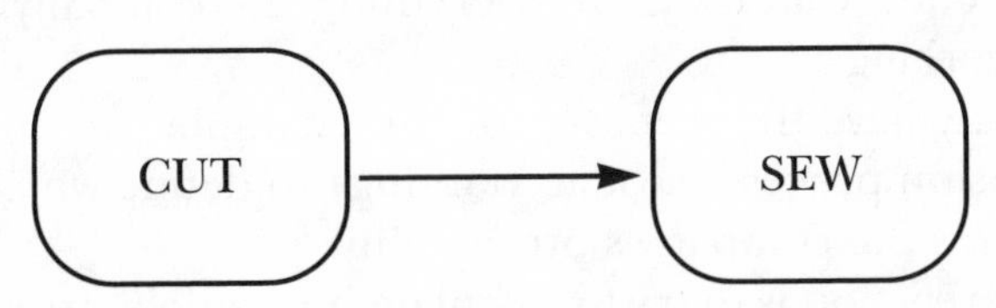

First we have to cut and then we sew the pieces together. The company makes only two different kinds of shirts, one for women and another for men.

The women's shirt is cut in 2 minutes on the cutting machine and then it is sewn in 15 minutes on the sewing machine. The men's shirt is cut in 10 minutes and sewn in 10 minutes. Below is the table showing each shirt's data:

Table 2-1

	Women's	**Men's**
Weekly Demand	120	120
Price	105	100
Raw Material Cost	45	50
Cutting Time	2	10
Sewing Time	15	10
Total Process Time	17	20

Both, women's and men's shirts, have a weekly demand of 120 units. The selling price is US$ 105 for women's and US$ 100 for men's shirts.

To sell one women's shirt we need to buy a Raw Material 1 (RM1 - fabric), for US$ 45. The men's shirt is composed of Raw Material 2 (RM2 - another fabric). The process sequence is the same for both products, what differs is the process time, the raw material cost and the selling price.

Each machine has an operator, and all the operators work 8 hours a day, 5 days a week, which adds up to 2,400 minutes a week. The investment and the cost for each resource are the same. The company's weekly operating expenses are US$ 10,500 (which include rents, energy and wages), everything the company spends to keep itself working.

We already have the scenario for this example. We now need to use our decision process (cost accounting) to define which product mix maximizes the company's profitability.

The first reaction is to try to calculate how much profit we would make if we sold all the demand for both products. But, the company does not have enough capacity to produce 120 women's shirts and 120 men's shirts in one week. The sewing machine does not have enough capacity (see the following table).

Table 2-2

Resource	Minutes necessary for women's shirt	Minutes necessary for men's shirt	Total minutes necessary	Necessary minutes/available minutes
Cutting	240	1,200	1,440	60%
Sewing	**1,800**	**1,200**	**3,000**	**125%**

We cannot sell everything the market wants to buy, therefore we need to decide what we will produce and sell. In this case, to maximize the company's profitability, we need to know which product is more profitable in order to produce as much of it that the market demands, and only then, if there is any time left on the sewing machine to produce the other product.

Nowadays we use cost accounting as the tool to calculate which products contribute the most to the company's profitability. Therefore, let us find out which product is most profitable according to this methodology.

To calculate the cost of a product we need its raw material costs and we need to add up the costs to produce this product (how much time it uses each resource, how much each resource costs, how much of the indirect costs should be allocated to each product, and so on.) We are not going to go into much detail on the mechanics of the process; the important thing here is to realize that the cost of a product is the consequence of how much it uses of each resource of the company.

To find out the profit per product we need to subtract the product cost from its price.

Table 2-3

	Women's shirt	Men's shirt	Best product
Price	US$ 105	US$ 100	women's
Raw Material	US$ 45	US$ 50	women's
Process Time	17 minutes	20 minutes	women's

The preceding table shows that the women's shirt is superior to the men's shirt in all the characteristics. It has a lower raw material cost, it uses less time of the company's resources and it has a higher price. This makes it the most profitable product, no matter what cost system is adopted.

As we do not have enough capacity to make all the products, and we want to have the highest possible profit, we must first sell all the demand of the most profitable product, and then, if there is any time left on the sewing machine, make the other product.

We will make all the demand for women's shirts (the most profitable product) –120 units. As every women's shirt uses 15 minutes of the sewing machine, to produce 120 units we will use 1,800 minutes. We have 2,400 minutes available, therefore we will have 600 minutes left, which we will use making men's shirts. As each men's shirt uses 10 minutes of the sewing machine, we can make 60 units. Then, the product mix that maximizes the company's profit is: 120 women's shirts + 60 men's shirts. Now let us calculate our profit from this mix.

Table 2-4

	US$
Revenue	$18,600
Raw Material Cost	$8,400
Gross Margin	$10,200
Operating Expense	–$10,500
Net Profit	–$300

As such, 120 women's shirts, at US$ 105 each, generate sales of US$ 12,600. And 60 men's shirts, at US$ 100 each, generate sales of US$ 6,000. With this mix the company has a total of US$ 18,600 in sales. The raw material costs of the 120 women's shirts are US$ 5,400 (120 x US$ 45), the raw material costs of the 60 men's shirts are US$ 3,000 (60 x US$ 50), which adds up to a total of US$ 8,400 in raw material costs. Thus the company has a gross margin (Sales – Raw material) of US$ 10,200. Its weekly operating expense is US$ 10,500, which results in a net profit of –US$ 300 (net loss).

Following this reasoning, the maximum this company can generate is a weekly loss of US$ 300. Our only option is to close the company. But, before making such a radical decision, let us leave aside the information supplied by cost accounting and let us examine what would happen to the company's profit if we sold all the demand for men's shirts (the least profitable) and only then sold part of the demand for women's shirts (the most profitable).

We will make all the demand for men's shirts, 120 units. As every men's shirt uses up 10 minutes of the sewing machine, to produce 120 units we will use 1,200 minutes. We have 2,400 minutes available, therefore we will have 1,200 minutes left, which we will use making women's shirts. As each women's shirt uses 15 minutes of the sewing machine, we can make 80 units. The company's new product mix is: 80 women's shirts + 120 men's shirts. Now let us calculate our profit.

Table 2-5

	US$
Revenue	$20,400
Raw Material Costs	$9,600
Gross Margin	$10,800
Operating Expense	–$10,500
Net Profit	$300

As a result, 80 women's shirts, at US$ 105 each, generate sales of US$ 8,400. 120 men's shirts, at US$ 100 each, generate sales of US$ 12,000. With this mix the company has a total of US$ 20,400 in sales. The raw material costs for the 80 women's shirts are US$ 3,600 (80 x US$ 45), the raw material costs for the 120 men's shirts are US$ 6,000 (120 x US$ 50), which adds up to a total of US$ 9,600 in raw material costs. Thus the company has a gross margin of US$ 10,800. Its weekly operating expense is of US$ 10,500, which results in a net profit of US$ 300.

We did not change anything in the company's conditions, yet we went from a loss of US$ 300 to a profit of US$ 300 a week! Cost accounting did not supply the correct information about which product most contributes to the company's profit. We increased the production of the least profitable product while decreasing the production of the most profitable product and our profits increased.

The only logical conclusion is that there is an error in cost accounting.

In our example we had only two products and two resources, which makes it easy to find out which mix generates the highest profit (by trial and error). But what do we do in a company with hundreds or even thousands of products and resources?

Up until now we saw that cost accounting gave us incorrect information (ranking of products according to profitability), which led us to a wrong decision. But if there is an error in this methodology, other information can be wrong as well.

2.1.1. Minimizing Product Costs

To illustrate the magnitude of the flaws in cost accounting let us use another example. Cost accounting tries to minimize products' costs. This happens because cost accounting is based on the assumption that the lower the cost of a product, the greater a company's profit. As the product cost results from the products' use of the company's resources, one way of reducing the cost of a product is by reducing its process time on a resource.

In the case of 2Shirt company, let us analyze a reduction in the process time of men's shirts in the cutting machine. Right now the men's shirt uses 10 minutes of the cutting machine, but if we invest US$ 100 we can reduce this time to 8 minutes.

By doing this we will reduce this product's total processing time from 20 to 18 minutes, a 10% reduction, and for this we only need to invest US$ 100. Cost accounting will surely approve of this investment.

What impact would this have on the company's profit?

To answer this question we need to know the impact this decision will have on the company's sales. Are we going to sell more products? No, after all the sewing machine establishes how much we can sell, and we did not change this resource's capacity.

Where did this decision have any impact? It increased the company's investment by US$ 100, therefore it also increased the company's cost (depreciation of this investment).

In the end, sales were not affected, and there was an increase in investment and in cost. This means that profitability decreased.

To confuse you even further, let us analyze another case. Someone suggested an investment of US$ 1,000, to decrease the women's shirt sewing time by 1 minute on the sewing machine, and at the same time increase by 3 minutes its time on the cutting machine. In other words, increase the process time of women's shirt by 2 minutes, and spend US$ 1,000 to do so. In cost accounting this would result in an increase of the product's cost, and, obviously, it would never be accepted.

What impact would this have on the company's profit?

To answer this question we need to know the impact this decision will have on the company's sales. Are we going to sell more products? Yes, because now each women's shirt spends 1 minute less on the sewing machine. As the sewing machine establishes how much the company is going to produce, we will be able to increase the quantity produced.

To quantify this impact we are going to use the mix that resulted in a profit of US$ 300. That mix is: 80 women's shirts + 120 men's shirts. This mix utilized 100% of the sewing machine's time. Now the women's shirt uses 1 minute less of the sewing machine's time, and therefore there are 80 more minutes of sewing time to be used to produce more women's shirts.[4] Therefore, we can increase the supply of women's shirts (which have a weekly demand of 120 units). Each woman's shirt uses 14 minutes of the sewing machine's time, and as we have 80 additional minutes, we can produce 5.7 women's shirts more a week.

The new product mix is: 85 women's shirts + 120 men's shirts. Now let us calculate our profit.

[4] Each women's shirt uses 14 minutes of the sewing machine's time. So 80 women's shirts use 1,120 minutes. Each men's shirt uses 10 minutes of sewing time. So 120 men's shirts use 1,200 minutes. As a result, 1,120 + 1,200 = 2,320. Available capacity = 2,400 minutes. Thus, we still have 80 minutes left.

Table 2-6

	US$
Revenue	$20,925
Raw Material Costs	$9,825
Gross Margin	$11,100
Operating Expense[5]	–$10,500
Net Profit	$600

The profit went from US$ 300 a week to US$ 600.

Remember what we did. We increased the process time of a product, and consequently, increased its cost, and by doing that we doubled the company's profit. And do not forget that if we had followed cost accounting we would not have approved this investment. As a matter of fact we would have approved the investment that decreases the company's profit.

Cost accounting is not capable of giving good information because it assumes that all the company's resources are equally important. It is as if we were trying to increase a chain's resistance by strengthening any link. We all know that a chain's resistance is determined by its weakest link, which means that we can only increase its resistance by increasing its weakest link's resistance. But cost accounting does not view the company as a system: that is why it does not differentiate between the company's resources (we will analyze this more deeply in other chapters).

We have had enough examples for now. I am assuming that you have been convinced that there is a fundamental flaw in cost accounting. Let us now try to understand a little bit better why cost accounting makes these mistakes, and let us see how this methodology developed.

[5] As a matter of fact the company's operating expense will increase, due to the investment made. But this increase will be so small that I did not include it in this analysis.

2.2. Cost Accounting's Paradigm

Let us try to understand how and why cost accounting was created, so that we can understand why it has become obsolete.[6]

A company's *net profit* is formed by the sum of the products' revenues (Rp), minus the sum of these products' raw material costs (RMp), minus the sum of the company's operating expenses. The operating expenses are divided into various categories, like wages, rent and taxes (OEc).

Hence, the formula is: $NP = \sum Rp - \sum RMp - \sum OEc$

In the above formula, the first two totals are done on the basis of products, while the third is based on categories of expenses.

In the beginning of the century, companies were starting to internalize many processes, and that demanded answers to new questions. The most important questions were those related to the impact a product had on the company's performance. What is the impact of a product on the company's total costs and revenues? The allocation of the OE to the various products was created to be able to quickly answer this type of very important question and to be able to make local decisions that would result in global optimization.

This solution simplified the situation by going from two different divisions—products and categories of expenses—to only one division. This was an alternate division of the operating expenses, not by categories, but by products. It was not exact, as not all the expenses were totally variable in relation to the production volume, but it was an approximation sufficiently reasonable to provide good information.

The expenses that could not be divided by products were all grouped together and then were allocated to the products according to the contribution of direct workers. Remember that these expenses were not significant overall. Thus, all expenses were divided by products, exactly like the revenues and the raw material costs. In this way the mathematical model became much simpler:

$$NP = \sum Rp - \sum RMp - \sum OEp$$
$$NP = \sum p \ (R\text{-}RM\text{-}OE)p$$

This formula enabled managers to analyze product by product individually, calculating each product's cost and profit. By doing this it became possible to analyze the company, product by product,

[6] This part of the chapter is based on the seventh chapter of *The Haystack Syndrome* by E. Goldratt.

thereby enabling managers to make decisions about one product without looking at other ones. With allocation, making decisions became easier.

However, the new found case in decision making was not the most important feature. The information was also of good quality, because the majority of the costs varied accordingly with the production volume, as the biggest part of cost was comprised of raw material and direct labor (which at that time was paid according to production volume). Therefore allocation made for a good approximation.

2.3. Obsolescence

Over the years, firm's cost structure changed significantly. Nowadays direct labor's participation in the total costs is decreasing; in many cases it is not more than 10%. Even so, most companies continue to use it as a base for allocation, that is, they still use direct labor as a base for allocating the overhead.

Many point to this factor as the cause for cost accounting's faulty information. The way it is being used, it only fulfills the goal of the external statements. Management accounting's real objective has been forgotten. We use distorted information and, consequently, make wrong decisions.

In addition, direct labor is no longer paid by the piece, and the overhead, which is the expenses allocated to the products, is now a company's most significant cost. This has made the allocation's approximation no longer acceptable.

Nowadays most of the expenses do not vary directly with the production volume, in most the cases only the raw material costs behave that way.

Management accounting tried to solve these problems by further developing the existing paradigm. It expanded the concepts of cost accounting creating more complex methodologies, which are still based on the same principles. Theorists assumed that what was wrong with management accounting was the fact that it allocated using only one activity measure—direct labor—and therefore they stipulated that many activity measures should be used.

"The use of only one activity measure, direct labor hours, reduces the ability of the cost system to predict the variation in cost with changes in the volume and mix of actual production."[7]

[7] JOHNSON and KAPLAN. *Relevance Lost,* p. 191.

Nowadays cost accounting does not allocate expenses based only on activity measures related to production volume. It also uses other activity measures, "besides recognizing that certain costs vary in proportion to the number of units produced, ABC also tries to identify the cost variability in relation to number of production batches, of the products maintenance activities in the market, changes in production's technology and methodology, sales and distribution of products etc." [8]

The new cost accounting methodologies assume that all costs are variable in relation to some activity, be it number of production batches, number of orders, or whatever. "The variable cost in ABC is an element of cost that varies with changes in the cost drivers' or activities' volume. For example, the cost of the activity to move materials varies accordingly with the number of times it is necessary to move the material from one activity to another."[9] If we vary the number of times we move materials will our costs vary? If we increase the number of times we move materials will we have to hire another person to do this? Or if we decrease the number of material moves will we fire someone? This does not sound very reasonable. Some ABC advocates have recently recognized that "the expense of supplying this resource is incurred, each period, independent of how much of the resource is used."[10] They also recognize that we should not make decisions based on this: "Making decisions based solely upon resource usage (the ABC system) is problematic because there is no guarantee that the spending to supply resources will be aligned with the new levels of resources demanded in the near future. . . . Consequently, before making decisions based on an ABC model, managers should analyze the resource supply implications of such decisions."[11] Even though they do recognize this, they still argue ABC is useful and necessary for long-term decisions (as we will see later on).

Cost accounting's obsolescence did not result because it only used one activity measure to allocate costs, but because it allocated costs to the products. The allocation's obsolescence came out

[8] NAKAGAWA, M. *ABC, Custeio Baseado em Atividades.* São Paulo: Atlas, 1994, p. 55.
[9] *Ibid.*
[10] KAPLAN, Robert S., COOPER, Robin. *Cost and Effect. Using Integrated Cost Systems to Drive Profitability and Performance.* Boston: Harvard Business School Press, 1998, p. 120.
[11] *Ibid.*, p. 125.

because the expenses that are allocated, in whatever allocation system, do not vary directly with production volume and/or mix, or with any other variable. Hence, the allocation only confuses us and causes us to make irrational decisions. As I will show in this book, cost allocation, whatever method used, does not reveal the impact of a decision on the bottom-line.

This brings us to two questions:

- Can we still change cost methods so that they can give us good information?
- Do we need to allocate costs to products?

Here is a first attempt to answer the first question: Allocation is not able to give us good information anymore, because it is based on erroneous assumptions.

> The cost concept is based on the assumption that 'we can measure the impact of a local area (or local decision) on the bottom line, by measuring how much money this area (or decision) absorbs or releases.' This assumption holds only if we accept that the importance of all things in an organization are in proportion to the operating expense spent on them. Daily life teaches us the opposite. Take for example a case where we run out of a specific material. The damage to the system might be out of proportion to the cost of this material.[12]

The second question has a slightly different meaning. The point is, even if more complicated allocation methods can give better information, do we need them? Might there be a simpler way to make good decisions? If that simpler way exists, then, even if allocation methods give good information, we would not need them.

I will deal first with the second question. The next chapters will discuss TOC's solution to management accounting, showing that it is very simple and that it provides good information. After that I will answer in more depth the first question.

[12] GOLDRATT, Eliyahu. *The Theory of Constraints Journal,* volume 1, number 2, April/May 1988. Avraham Y. Goldratt Institute, p. 19.

3
Theory of Constraints (TOC)

3.1. History

TOC began in the 70's, when the Israeli physicist, Eliyahu Goldratt, got involved with the problems of production logistics. Goldratt did not have any background in business, but he used the methods of problem-solving he learned in physics to try and solve the problems of production logistics.

Goldratt created a completely new method of production logistics, even though he had no prior knowledge of the existing methods. He was intrigued by the fact that traditional production methodologies did not make any logical sense.

His method was very successful, and many companies were interested. Goldratt then dedicated himself to developing it further and to disseminating it. In the beginning of the 80's he wrote a book about his theory. The book, *The Goal*, was written in the form of a novel and shows the difficulty of a plant manager's struggles to run the business. As the story goes on, the manager starts to discover the principles of Goldratt's theory and the company regains competitiveness. The book's success was, and still is, enormous. Many managers read the book and started applying TOC's principles. In the book, Goldratt criticizes traditional management methods, including cost accounting.

Many companies that were implementing Goldratt's production logistics increased their production's performance so much that problems started to appear in other areas. Goldratt created solutions to other areas, like distribution logistics and project management. But he knew that companies needed something more fundamental than ready-made solutions: Every time a company applied the solutions he had created they would increase their competitiveness, but would then stagnate.

He then decided to teach the logical reasoning that he used to solve problems. He believes that companies need to know how to solve their own problems so that they can guarantee their future, so that they can improve continuously. These logical reasoning tools, that he used intuitively, were made explicit in 1991 and have been taught since then by the Goldratt Institute.

Nowadays TOC is divided into two fields, the Thought Processes on one side, and the specific applications (like production logistics, developed using the Thought Processes) on the other. TOC's thought process have surpassed the limits of business management and are used in many other areas.

The basic assumption behind these thought processes is that, in any system, there are few causes that explain the many effects. The thought processes are based on the laws of cause and effect, they are logical diagrams that help us explicit our intuition. They are comprised of five tools: the Current Reality Tree (CRT), the Evaporating Cloud (EC), the Future Reality Tree (FRT), the Pre-Requisite Tree (PRT) and the Transition Tree (TT). These five tools can be used together or separately, depending on the desired objective. As more people use the thought process, new uses for them emerge.[13]

This background on TOC explains why many people still view it as merely a production-related application. *The Goal*, which has been TOC's main promoter up to now, is based on the problems of production logistics, while the Thought Processes appeared some time after and still have not been as widely promoted and/or implemented.

To try to overcome this obstacle in the dissemination of TOC as a whole, Goldratt wrote, in 1994, another book *It's Not Luck* (using the same style he used in *The Goal*). The story resolves around the more strategic problems of the company, using the thought processes.

In the 80's, Goldratt accused cost accounting of being the number-one enemy of productivity. As a result TOC gained many opponents, but Goldratt also caught the attention of those people who no longer believed in cost accounting as the best supplier of information for decision-making.

[13] For more information on TOC's Thought Processes, read two books by Eliyahu Goldratt: *What Is This Thing Called the Theory of Constraints and How Should It Be Implemented?* and *It's Not Luck* as well as H. William Dettmer's *Goldratt's Theory of Constraints: A System's Approach to Continuous Improvement.*

3.2. Basic Concepts

In this study we will be dealing with managerial accounting for industries, so we will first get a brief overview of TOC's basic concepts for production logistics[14] and then see how TOC's managerial accounting fits this context.

TOC is based on the principle that there is a common cause for many effects, that the effects we see and feel are a consequence of deeper causes. This principle leads us to a systemic view of the company.

TOC sees any company as a system, that is, a set of elements in an interdependent relationship. Each element depends on the others in some way, and the global performance of the system depends on the joint efforts of all the elements of the system. One of the most fundamental concepts is the recognition of the important role played by the system's constraint.

> The first step is to recognize that every system was built for a purpose, we did not create our organizations just for the sake of their existence. Thus, every action taken by any organ—any part of the organization—should be judged by its impact on the overall purpose. This immediately implies that, before we can deal with the improvement of any section of a system, we must first define the system's global goal; and the measurements that will enable us to judge the impact of any subsystem and any local decision, on this global goal. . . . A system's constraint is nothing more than what we feel to be expressed by these words: **anything that limits a system from achieving higher performance versus its goal**. . . . In our reality any system has very few constraints (this is what is proven in *The Goal*, by the boy-scout analogy) and at the same time any system in reality must have at least one constraint.[15]

The assertion that every system has to have at least one constraint is explained by the fact that if there were nothing limiting the

[14] We examine these concepts very briefly. For more information, read: *The Race*, *Self-Learning Kit* and *Synchronous Manufacturing. Principles for World-class Excellence* by M. Srikanth and M. Umble.

[15] GOLDRATT, Eliyahu. *What Is This Thing Called the Theory of Constraints and How Should It Be Implemented?* Croton-on-Hudson: North River Press, 1990, p. 4, my emphasis.

system's performance, then it would be infinite. If a company did not have a constraint, its profit would be infinite.

TOC's process of ongoing improvement resulted from this reasoning, always focusing all efforts towards the system's goal. This process is the basis for TOC's methodologies, including its methodology for management accounting. This process has five steps:

1. **Identify** the System's Constraint(s).
2. Decide how to **Exploit** the System's Constraint(s).
3. **Subordinate** everything else to the above decision.
4. **Elevate** the System's Constraint(s).
5. If in the previous steps a Constraint has been broken, go back to Step 1. **But Do Not Allow Inertia to Cause a System Constraint.**

1. Identify the System's Constraint(s).

In a plant there will always be a resource that limits its maximum flow,[16] as in a chain there always is a weakest link. In order to increase the system's performance, to increase the chain's resistance, we must identify the weakest link. In a plant the resources that establish the maximum flow are called Capacity Constraint Resource (CCR).[17]

"Once this is accomplished . . . the next step becomes self evident. We have just put our fingers on the few things which are in short supply, short to the extent that they limit the entire system. So let's make sure that we don't waste the little that we have."[18] In other words, Step two is as follows.

2. Decide How to Exploit the System's Constraint(s).

We have identified the resource that limits the plant's performance. Now we need to get the most out of it. Any minute lost on this resource is a minute lost in the system's production level, so we need to guarantee that there will always be a security buffer in front of the constraint so that it will not stop due to lack of material.

[16] Depending on the complexity and the process flow, there might be more than one resource that limits the output of the plant. The best analogy for these plants is a net of chains. Even so, there will be very few resources that limit the system's performance.

[17] The CCR is only the company's constraint if its capacity is equal to or smaller than the market's demand, that is, if the market wants to buy more than it can produce.

[18] GOLDRATT, E. *What Is This Thing Called the Theory of Constraints, and How Should It Be Implemented?* p. 5.

> Now that we decided how we are going to manage the constraints, how should we manage the vast majority of the system's resources, which are not constraints? Intuitively it's obvious. We should manage them so that everything that the constraints are going to consume will be supplied by the non-constraints. Is there any point in managing the non-constraints to supply more than that? This of course will not help, since the overall system's performance is sealed-dictated by the constraints.[19]

3. Subordinate Everything Else to the Above Decision.

The other resources should work at the constraint's pace, neither faster or slower. They cannot let the constraint run out of material to process, because then it would stop and the system's performance would be jeopardized. On the other hand, the non-constraint resources should not work faster than the constraint because they would not be increasing the system's production level, they would only be increasing the level of work in process.

"But let's not stop here, it's obvious we still have room for much more improvement. Constraints are not acts of God, there is much that we can do about them. Whatever the constraints are, there must be a way to reduce their limiting impact and thus the next step to concentrate on, is quite evident."[20]

4. Elevate the System's Constraint(s).

In the second step we tried to get the most out of the constraint. In this one we consider the many alternatives for investing on the constraint: more shifts, another identical resource . . .

> Can we stop here? Yes, your intuition is right. There will be another constraint, but let's verbalize it a little bit better. If we elevate and continue to elevate a constraint, then there must come a time when we break it. This thing that we have elevated will no longer be limiting the system. Will the system's performance now go to infinity? Certainly not. Another constraint will limit its performance and thus the fifth step must be [as follows].[21]

[19] *Ibid.*
[20] *Ibid.*
[21] *Ibid.*, p. 6

5. If in the Previous Steps a Constraint Has Been Broken, Go Back to Step 1.

> Unfortunately, we cannot state these five steps without adding to the last one, a warning; 'But Do Not Allow Inertia to Cause a System Constraint.'
>
> We cannot overemphasize this warning. What usually happens is that within our organization, we derive from the existence of the current constraints, many rules. Sometimes formally, many times just intuitively. When a constraint is broken, it appears that we don't bother to go back and review those rules. As a result, our systems today are limited mainly by policy constraints.[22]

One of the main assumptions behind TOC is that every system, like a for-profit company, has to have at least one constraint. Therefore, if we want to better the system's performance we need to manage its constraint(s). "There really is no choice in this matter. Either you manage constraints or they manage you. The constraints will determine the output of the system whether they are acknowledged and managed or not."[23]

The constraints are not intrinsically good or bad, they simply exist. If you choose to ignore them they can become bad. If you choose to recognize and manage them they become a great opportunity, a real leverage for your business.

3.3. Performance Measurements

According to Goldratt, "before we can deal with the improvement of any section of a system, we must first define the system's global goal; and the measurements that will enable us to judge the impact of any subsystem and any local decision, on this global goal."[24]

We have already determined that the company's goal is to make

[22] *Ibid.*

[23] NOREEN, Eric and SMITH, Debra and MACKEY, James T. *The Theory of Constraints and its Implications for Management Accounting.* Great Barrington: North River Press, 1995. p. xix.

[24] GOLDRATT, E. *What Is . . .* p. 4

money now and in the future. To make the bridge between NP and ROI, TOC uses three measurements. The measurements have to be purely financial, to show if the company is going toward its goal or not. To judge if a company is moving toward its goal we must answer "Three simple questions: How much money is generated by our company? How much money is captured by our company? And how much money do we have to spend to operate it?[25] The measurements are intuitively obvious. What is needed is to turn these questions into formal definitions."[26]

TOC's measurements are:

- **Throughput (T):** the rate at which the system generates money through sales.
- **Investment (I):** all the money the system invests in purchasing items the system intends to sell.
- **Operating Expense (OE):** all the money the system spends in turning investment into throughput.

> *Throughput*—The rate at which the system generates money.
>
> As a matter of fact, we will get a more precise definition if we will erase the last two words—through sales. You see, if the system generates money by earning interest at a bank, it is definitely throughput. Why did I add these two words? Because of a common behavior in our companies. Most production managers think that if they have produced something, it deserves to be called throughput. . . . Throughput cannot possibly be associated with shuffling money internally. Throughput means to bring fresh money from the outside, thus the additional words—through sales.[27]

Throughput is defined as all the money that comes into the company minus what it paid to its vendors. This is the money the company generated, the money paid to the vendors is money generated by other companies.

[25] To get an idea of how these three questions show if a particular decision takes the company toward its goal, see chapter 4 of *The Goal.*
[26] GOLDRATT, Eliyahu. *The Haystack Syndrome, Sifting Information Out of the Data Ocean.* Croton-on-Hudson: North River Press, 1990, p. 19.
[27] *Ibid.*

The formulas to calculate throughput are the following:

Tu = P – TVC
where: Tu = Throughput per unit of product
P = Price per unit of product
TVC = **Totally** Variable Cost, that is, the amount of cost that varies for every increase in the product's sale (in the majority of the cases it is just raw material)

TTp = Tu x q
where: TTp = Total Throughput per product
q = Quantity sold in the period

Company's Total Throughput = ΣTTp

Example: A company has two products, P and Q.

Table 3-1

	P	**Q**
Price (P)	90	100
TVC	45	40
Quantity Sold (q)	100	50
Tu (P – TVC)	45	60
TTp (Tu x q)	4,500	3,000

ΣTTp = 7,500

Throughput has two sides, the *Revenue* and the *Totally Variable Costs (TVC)*. The use of the words *variable* and *cost* may confuse us with the measures used in cost accounting. The fundamental element here, without any doubt, is the word *Totally* — Totally variable in relation to the units sold. A TVC is that amount incurred when one more product is sold. The obvious example is raw material costs; for each extra unit sold the company incurs the value of the raw material of that product. Other things may be classified as TVC, depending on the nature of the operation. If the cost variation is directly proportional to the variation in production volume, then it is a TVC, and it should be subtracted from the product's selling price to calculate its throughput.

Investment[28]—All the money the system invests in purchasing items the system intends to sell. This measurement and the conventional accounting measurement assets might be mistaken, but they actually differ drastically when referring to work in process and finished goods inventory.

> What value should we attach to a finished product stored in a warehouse? According to the definition given above, we are allowed to assign just the price that we paid to our vendors for the material and purchased parts that went into the product. There is no added value by the system itself, not even direct labor.[29]

The value ascribed to the *work in process* (WIP) and the *finished goods inventory* is their TVC. One of the objectives here is to eliminate the generation of "apparent profits" due to the cost allocation process. With this methodology it is not possible to increase short-term profits by increasing WIP and finished goods inventory (delaying the recognition of some expenses that will certainly decrease profits of future periods).

According to this measurement we classify the company's buildings, such as land, computers, furniture, cars, machines and trucks. The definition of this measurement might cause some confusion: "All the money the system invests in purchasing things the system intends to sell." Do the companies intend to sell their machines, buildings and so on? If we examine this question from the stockholder's perspective, if the company does not generate the expected profitability he will sell his stocks, which is the same as selling his part of the machines, buildings and so on.

The investment should be divided into two categories: (1) the inventory of raw material, and (2) work in process and finished goods and the other assets. This is because the inventory of materials has a great impact on the company's competitiveness, as we will see later on.

Operating Expense—All the money the system spends in turning investment into throughput. "Taking added value out of inventory does not mean that we do not have these outlays of money."[30] There

[28] Goldratt calls this measurement "inventory".

[29] GOLDRATT, E. *The Haystack*, p. 23.

[30] *Ibid.*, p. 29.

is no value added to the product. Operating Expense (OE) is intuitively understood as all the money we have to pour into the machine on an ongoing basis to turn the machine's wheels."[31] Wages, from the company's CEO to the direct labor, rents, energy, etc. TOC does not classify expenses as fixed, variable, indirect or direct. OE is all other costs other than totally variable costs. The increases or decreases in OE are analyzed on a case-by-case basis, and their impact on the bottom line is taken into account.

The most common error is to think that TOC regards OE as fixed. TOC does not care about classifying expenses as fixed or semi-variable; what really matters is whether they are totally variable or not totally variable. When we are making a decision we need to measure the impact on the three measurements. At this time we must analyze whether OE will vary or not, always on a case-by-case basis.

TOC says that these three measurements are sufficient for us to bridge the gap between NP and ROI and the managers' daily actions. Below are the formulas that demonstrate this bridge:

$$NP = T - OE$$

$$ROI = (T - OE)/I$$

where: T = Total Throughput, ΣTTp

OE = Total Operating Expense

I = Total Investment

With these three measurements (T, I and OE) we can figure out the impact of a decision on the company's bottom line. The ideal is a decision that increases T and decreases I and OE. However, any decision that has a positive impact on ROI is a decision that takes the company towards its goal. The final judge, the one who decides if it is a good decision or not, is ROI.

We do not need to calculate the NP for the entire company, nor the ROI. We can calculate the incremental NP and ROI. If they are positive and if the ROI is equal to or greater than a predetermined percentage, then the decision is a good one.

3.4. Priorities in TOC

Use the chain analogy to exemplify some of TOC's principles. If we pull a chain, where will it break? At its weakest link (only **one**

[31] *Ibid.*, p. 18.

link). If this chain's goal is to resist traction, where should we concentrate to better its performance? We should strengthen its weakest link, this system's constraint. Strengthening any other link before strengthening the weakest one would be a waste of time and resources, because the weakest link determines the maximum performance of the entire chain. That is why the first step in a process of ongoing improvement has to be: Identify the system's constraint(s) (the weakest link).

A plant is very similar to a chain. As an example let us use company XYZ, which has a very simple process, with five operations (figure 3-1), and whose market is overheated. The raw material enters the process at resource A, and is processed in sequence until resource E, where the finished product is ready to be sold. The number within each operation is the average capacity of each resource in parts/hour. This company sells only one product (X), with a price of US$ 100 and a raw material cost of US$ 35, which gives a throughput per unit of US$ 65. The company's resources work 8 hours a day, 22 days a month, that is, 176 hours a month.

Figure 3-1: XYZ plant

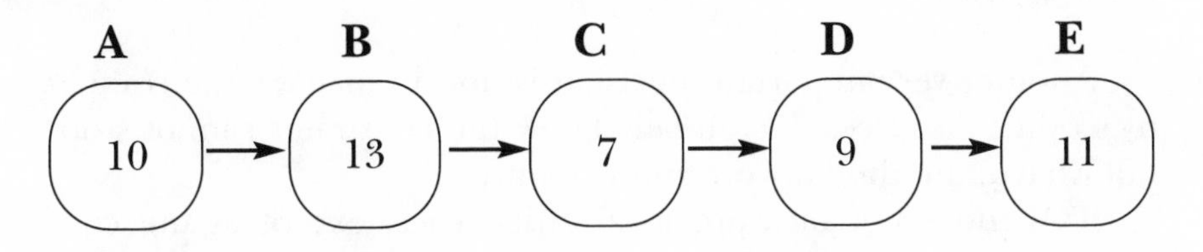

Resource C limits the plant's capacity; it is the Capacity Constraint Resource (CCR), the weakest link. C limits the performance of this company to 7 parts per hour, which gives the company a total throughput of US$ 80,080 a month.[32] To increase the plant's performance we must focus our efforts on resource C. Improving the performance of the other links will not have an impact on the system's performance, and many times such improvements can be counter productive.

Let us use TOC's three measurements (T, I and OE) to analyze these statements, and to see how we should evaluate decisions according to TOC.

[32] 176 hours x 7 parts an hour = 1,232 parts a month. Monthly Throughput = 1,232 x 65 = US$ 80,080.

Someone made a proposal to optimize resource B, bettering its performance from 13 to 14 parts per hour, which requires an investment of US$ 5,000. We must then quantify the impact of accepting this proposal on the company's goal, and calculate the impact on T, I and OE.

Throughput will not increase because the plant can only produce 7 parts per hour, although the investment will increase by US$ 5,000 and Operating Expenses will increase by US$ 41.67 a month[33] due to the depreciation of this investment. As T did not increase, NP decreases according to the depreciation, that is, NP decreases US$ 41.67 a month, so the ROI of this investment is negative. Therefore, the company decides not to approve this project.

Another project was presented. Resource C is optimized, and goes from 7 to 7.1 parts per hour, but resource E has an extra load, and goes from 11 to 10 parts per hour. The investment necessary is US$ 5,000.

The company's throughput will increase by US$ 1,144 a month,[34] Operating Expense will increase by US$ 41.67 a month and the investment will increase by US$ 5,000. Thus, the Net Profit will increase by US$ 1,102.33 a month, and this investment's ROI will be 265% a year.[35]

Another very important decision is how to manage the company's other resources. We already know the constraint cannot stop, but what about the nonconstraint resources?

TOC does not measure local efficiencies, except at the constraint. In this example, the nonconstraint resources would have idle time if managed according to TOC's principles. For the first resource, A, to have 100% efficiency, we would have to feed it with 10 parts per hour of raw material. This would not increase throughput (which is limited by resource C at 7 parts per hour). However, this would increase the investment, as the WIP would be increasing at a 3 part per hour rate. If the investment increases, so does OE, because of the costs to carry this extra Inventory. In this way, the search for

[33] US$ 5,000, depreciated at a 10% rate a year = US$ 500. A month = 500/12 = US$ 41.67.

[34] Increase in production = 0.1 parts an hour. Increase in the total production of parts in a month = 176 hours x 0.1 parts = 17.60 parts. Increase in the company's throughput = 17.60 parts x US$ 65 = US$ 1,144 a month.

[35] Annual increase in the NP = US$ 1,102.33 x 12 = US$ 13,227.96. ROI = US$ 13,227.96 ÷ US$ 5,000 = 265%.

local efficiency at the nonconstraint resources takes the company in the opposite direction of its goal! We can therefore conclude that idleness by the nonconstraint resources is a necessity. That is why the third step in TOC's process of ongoing improvement is to subordinate everything else to the decision of how to exploit the constraint.

Subordinating means rigorously demanding what the constraint needs (as decided in step 2) and nothing more. The nonconstraint resources need to guarantee the constraint's supply, and nothing else. They would not contribute to the company's goal if they produced 100% of their time. On the contrary, they would decrease the bottom line. The constraint establishes the production rhythm. The raw material release is controlled by the constraint's rhythm. Only what is programmed in the constraint is released, in order to avoid an increase in WIP, and consequently, an increase of the investment and in the OE.

To calculate the impact of the decisions on TOC's three measurements, we must understand the constraint's influence on these measurements.

For the throughput to increase we must increase the price and/or the quantity sold and/or decrease the TVC. The system's constraint has a fundamental role in increasing throughput.

To decrease I we must sell something the company bought, without increasing other investments. In this case all the elements of the system can affect this measurement.

To decrease OE we must diminish spending. Again, any element of the system can affect this measurement.

The few constraints in the system establish its throughput, and therefore, to increase T it is necessary to affect a system's constraint. The other two measurements can be affected by any link of the chain.

These three measurements offer managers a different prioritization. The most important measurement is T. The goal is always to increase T, and therefore, it is the only measurement of the three that does not have a limit. Investment and OE have to be decreased, and therefore have a limit, which is zero.

Moreover, focusing on T forces managers to think about the company as a whole, because you can only increase T by optimizing a system's constraint, and to identify the constraints of the system, it is necessary to have a global view. Focusing on T helps managers avoid trying to optimize their part of the system without taking into account the goal of the entire system.

As we can see, TOC does not calculate the products' costs. Goldratt says it is not necessary to do so. ". . . constraints are the essential classification, replacing the role that products played . . .",[36] "We have to evaluate the impact, not of a product, but of a decision".[37] According to Goldratt, when you have to make a decision, all you need to do is answer the following three questions: How much will T change? How much will I change? How much will OE change?

Now, in order to answer these questions, especially the first one, we need to understand the relation between the system's constraint and the company's products.

In the case of company XYZ, the production capacity of a machine is the constraint of the system; this is what is limiting the system from making more money. Resource C's minutes are very precious to the company, because any waste of time means diminished sales.

To clarify this let's go back to figure 3-1. Resource C, with an average capacity of 7 parts per hour, is the system's constraint. Assuming it works 40 hours[38] a week, the company is able to produce and sell 280 products[39] a week. This is the case only if the resource does not break or stop due to lack of material. However we know resources stop processing, for various reasons. Thus, when resource C stops, each minute lost means a decrease in throughput. If in a week resource C stops for an hour, the company will only be able to sell 273 products,[40] which decrease the throughput and Net Profit by US$ 455.

This is why the second step in TOC's ongoing improvement process is "to exploit the system's constraint(s)". Preventing the constraint from stopping becomes a priority. We need to put a buffer of stock in front of the constraint to guarantee its supply in case one of its feeding resources breaks down. However, leaving the constraint producing all the time is not enough; the constraint must produce the right things! When there is a constraint on the shop floor, you have to decide which products are most important, as the company does not have enough capacity to deliver all the products to the market in the amounts wanted.

[36] GOLDRATT, E. *The Haystack,* p. 57.
[37] *Ibid.,* p. 98.
[38] 8 hours a day, 5 days a week.
[39] 40 hours x 7 parts an hour = 280 parts.
[40] 39 hours x 7 parts an hour = 273 parts.

We need to keep in mind that the constraint is resource C's available time. To increase throughput the company needs to squeeze the most it can from this available time.

The constraint's available time is limited. Different products use the constraint's time differently. One product might need 5 minutes at the constraint while another needs half an hour. It is obvious that the one that uses less time should have a priority.

We also want to increase the company's throughput. Different products have different throughput. A product that has a throughput of US$ 100 should get priority over another product whose throughput is US$ 40.

As we can see, we want to give priority to products that have a greater throughput, and at the same time, give priority to products that use the least time at the constraint. We will have a problem when comparing two products—one has a greater throughput, while the other uses less time at the constraint. How do we decide which one is best for the company?

To solve this problem we need to adopt a relative measurement, which takes into account that we want to maximize throughput and at the same time minimize the time spent on the constraint.

On one hand we have the product's throughput, on the other the minutes it uses of the constraint. To decide which one contributes most to the company's bottom line we need to divide the product's throughput by the time it uses at the constraint, resulting in the product's throughput per time of the CCR. For example:

Table 3-2

Throughput/time on CCR	**Light**	**Heavy**
Throughput per unit (US$)	15	50
Minutes it uses of the CCR	2	10
Throughput/time of CCR (US$/minute)	**7.5**	**5**

In this case the company sells only two products: Light and Heavy. Light uses fewer minutes of the constraint than Heavy, but 'Heavy' has a greater throughput per unit. As the company does not have enough capacity to deliver all the orders, the managers have to decide which product is more important. Therefore we need to calculate the relationship between the throughput and the minutes used of the constraint. What this measurement tells us is that for every minute the constraint is producing Light the company's throughput increases US$ 7.5, and when it is producing Heavy the increase is US$ 5 per minute.

To better understand this measurement all you need to do is think as if the company is selling its most scarce resource, the minutes of the constraint. The products that better pay for the minutes they use are the ones that most contribute to the company's bottom line. In the above example, product Light 'pays' US$ 7.5 per minute and Heavy US$ 5 per minute. Therefore the company should give preference to Light, and only if the constraint has time left after producing all the demand for this product should it produce Heavy.

In the above example, one of the assumptions is that the market is bullish, that is, the market demands more than the company can produce. In this case, the throughput per time of the constraint makes sense. However, this is not always the case for all firms.

When the company has more capacity than the market demands, the constraint is the market. In this case the criteria for comparing products should be the throughput per unit, because there is no resource limiting the company's performance. The sale of any product whose price is bigger than TVC, and which does not increase OE, contributes to an increase in the bottom line. The assumption behind this analysis is that the company's OE does not vary proportionately with the production volume, especially if the company has idle capacity. "In TOC, the default assumption is that overhead functions, like other nonconstraint work centers, can handle additional diversity without new resources."[41]

TOC does not make any correlation between production volume, or any other variable of the system, with OE. The assumption is that the person making the decision is able to quantify the impact it will have on OE, and therefore, there is no need to try and discover, beforehand, any kind of relationship between OE and some variable of the system.

When the market demands more than the company can produce, TOC recommends using the throughput/time of constraint to see which products most contribute to the system's goal. That does not mean that the issues regarding marketing should be forgotten. Some products, even when not very important considering their throughput/time of CCR, have to be sold for marketing reasons.

[41] NOREEN, SMITH and MACKEY. *The Theory*, p. xxvii.

In any case, throughput/time of CCR or throughput/unit should not be considered alone when making a decision. Whatever the decision, it is necessary to quantify its impact on the three measurements, and on the company's NP and ROI, and for that we use the statements we will see in the next chapter.

3.5. Other Constraining Factors

The minutes of a resource are not the only possible physical constraint. Other factors can be constraining the flow of products or services, for example, direct labor hours, a specific raw material or a specific human skill.[42] Even though in these cases the minutes of a machine are not the constraint, the logic is still the same. We want to maximize the throughput and at the same time we want to minimize the use of the constraining factor. All we have to do is calculate the throughput/unit of the constraining factor. Thus, in the case the constraint is a specific raw material, we have to divide the product's throughput by the amount of units it uses of the raw material.

3.6. Conclusion

As we have seen, management accounting's objective is to make the connection between managers' local actions and the company's profitability so that they can know if their actions are leading the company towards its goal.

To do this TOC uses three measurements: throughput, investment and operating expense. To make a decision according to TOC, we need to quantify the decision's impact on these three measurements and then we will be able to see the increment in NP and ROI (and this will show us whether it is a good decision or not).

Throughput accounting is based on this basic assumption. "In The Goal only one assumption is postulated. The assumption that we can measure the goal of an organization by Throughput, Inventory and Operating Expenses. Everything else is derived logically from that assumption."[43]

The role of the company's constraint is fundamental for quantifying the decision's impact on the three measurements. Thus, to identify which products contribute the most to the company's bot-

[42] In many service companies this is the case. In consulting companies the constraining factor might be the senior consultants who have the necessary knowledge for the various projects.

[43] GOLDRATT, E. *What is . . .* p. 28.

tom line, TOC advocates the use of the measurement throughput/time of the CCR, when the capacity of this resource is lower than the market's demand. In this case, the throughput/time of the CCR and the decision's impact on OE substitute the product's cost. If the constraint is on the market's demand, that is, if all the company's resources have idle capacity then the throughput per unit and the decision's impact on OE substitute the product's cost.

As we have seen, this method is much simpler and is much more in line with the new view of the company than the costing methods. It allows for fast decisions and decisions that are directly linked to the bottom line. In the next chapter we will see examples of how to make decisions using these concepts, and we will also see the Throughput Accounting Statements.

4

Throughput Accounting Statements

Up until now we have seen a brief summary of TOC's concepts. In this chapter we will analyze some practical issues of this new management accounting. We will better understand such accounting statements, how they are built and how they should be used.

The statements analyzed here are generic; they are not adapted to the specificity of any one company.[44] Many companies already use them the way they are shown here, while others have made some changes. There is no right way to build these statements, and as long as TOC's principles are followed the company may adapt them to better supply their managers with information.

4.1. Basic Statements

Table 4-1 Operating Expense—Month xx

Item	US$
Wages	
Energy	
Rent	
Depreciation	
Interest	
Publicity	
Transport	
Others	
Total	

[44] The accounting statements shown here are based on the statements developed in 1988 by Allied Signal do Brasil - Garrett division.

Here is a statement of all the operating expenses for the period being analyzed.

Table 4-2
Data Base of the Products—Month xx

A	B	C	D (B-C)	E	F (D/E)
Product	**Price**	**TVC**	**Throughput per Unit (Tu)**	**Time on CCR**	**Throughput /Time on CCR**

Each of the company's products should be shown on this statement (column A), with its selling price (column B), its Totally Variable Cost (column C), its Throughput per Unit (Price – TVC, column D), the time it uses of the CCR (column E) and finally its throughput per time on CCR (Tu/time on CCR, column F). The products are presented in a decreasing manner according to their Tu/time on CCR, thus in a decreasing manner according to their contribution to the company's profitability.

When the company's constraint is not on a CCR, we do not need to use the throughput per time measurement, because in such a circumstance we do not have to decide what product to sell. The important factor then is each product's throughput and the impact of each decision on the company's OE.

The products that do not use any time of the CCR are called free products. For these products the demand is their constraint but the sales increase for these products should be done with a lot of criteria, because it can unbalance the production flow.[45]

To build this statement the company needs to have the data on its products' price, TVC and time on CCR; the other columns of Throughput per Unit and Throughput/time on CCR are a result of these data.

Product—In this column the company enters the product's code or name.

[45] For more details, see: *The Haystack Syndrome,* chapters 18 and 23.

Price—Here the company enters the product's selling price. Many companies sell the same product at different prices. Here we can have two cases. The first one is when the company sells at different prices to the same client. In this case the price should be a weighted average. The second case is when the company sells the same product at different prices to different clients. Then, the product should appear on this statement more than once (as many times as the number of different clients). In addition, it is important to identify in column A what client is getting what price, because a product might be very profitable when sold to a certain client and not very profitable when sold to another one. This can lead the company to decide to produce the product only for the client who pays a higher price.

Totally Variable Cost—In this column the company enters the product's Totally Variable Costs. Remember that TVC is that cost that varies directly with the production volume. If the company produces and sells another unit of the product it will incur this amount, and if it produces one unit less it will not incur this cost. The clearest example is raw material cost. Here we should include the scrap as part of TVC. If to produce 95 parts of a certain product it is necessary to feed the plant with 100 units, this should be included in the TVC. Other examples of TVC are packaging and in some cases transport and sales commissions (when they are a percent of the selling price).

Throughput per Unit—This results from subtracting the TVC from the selling price; it shows how much each unit of the product is contributing to the company's throughput.

Time on CCR—How much time does the product use of the CCR? In this case we need to add up the times that all the parts that comprise the final product use of the CCR. The time can be measured in minutes, seconds or hours. The important thing is to use the same unit for all products. This is the only process time that this methodology requires. We only need to have reliable data on the CCR; there is no need to have process times of any other resource.[46]

Throughput/Time on CCR—This results from the division of the

[46] It is important to remember that we do not need all the process times from all resources to identify the CCR. Usually the people who work in the plant have an intuition of what resource is the CCR. Apart from that, there are certain clues as to how to identify the CCR. For more information on this see *The Goal* and the *Self-Learning Kit.*

Throughput per Unit by the time the product uses of the CCR. This shows how much fresh money enters the company for every time unit that the CCR processes the product. This is the measurement that TOC uses to rank the product's profitability, as we saw in chapter 3.

The selling price, the TVC and the product's time on the CCR are the variables that can be manipulated to evaluate possible changes in the company (as we will see later on).

Having prepared this statement, the company can then forecast its financial performance according to the sales mix or even can do various simulations to see the impact of a decision on the company's bottom line. The statement used to do these forecasts and/or simulations is the following.

Table 4-3
Results

G	H	I	J	K		L (I or J x D)	
Product	**Demand (Forecast)**	**Maximum Throughput Mix**	**Sales Mix**	**Acum. Utiliz. of CCR %**		**Total Throughput per Product**	
	0	0	0	0.0%	0.0%	0	0
	0	0	0	0.0%	0.0%	0	0
	0	0	0	0.0%	0.0%	0	0

Maximum Profit Mix/Marketing Mix—Month xx

Capacity of CCR = Demand/CCR capacity =

Total Throughput	0	0
Operating Expense	0	0
Net Profit	0	0
(NP difference)	0	
Investment	0	0
ROI (annual)	0.0%	0.0%

In this statement we enter the sales forecast for each product and we accumulate the utilization time of the CCR and the total throughput for each product. If there is an internal constraint, the accumulated utilization of the CCR (column K) will be 100%. The products that are below the line where the accumulated utilization reached 100% will not be considered because of lack of capacity. We then add up the total throughput per product (column L), of all products that are contemplated on the CCR's available time, giving the company's maximum total throughput for the period being analyzed. From this value we subtract the company's OE and get its maximum net profit for the period.

Up until now we have calculated the maximum profit the company can generate in the period under analysis. In the majority of the cases the companies cannot impose a product mix on the market. What happens is that many products, even when not very profitable for the company, need to be sold to satisfy the market and to guarantee the company's future. Therefore, it is necessary to find a marketing mix, starting from the demand. In column J of this statement, the company should enter its sales mix, where the quantity to be produced and sold should never exceed the demand quantity of column H. If we have an CCR that is overloaded we need to decide what products we are not going to supply part or even all of the demand. Here there is no way out. In this statement the accumulated utilization (column K) cannot exceed 100%. This compels the company to make a decision about what clients and products are more important, always taking into account the financial aspects and the marketing aspects, as the company's goal is to make money now and in the future. Today many companies do not make this decision and end up promising to deliver to their clients when they do not have the capacity to do so, and this generates delays and unhappy clients, jeopardizing current and future profits.

In the columns that follow (K and L), we always have two divisions: the first one shows the mix of maximum profit mix and the second one shows the marketing mix results. After the Net Profit calculation for both situations, we have the calculation of the difference between the NP of these two mixes. This shows how much of our current profit we are giving up to guarantee the company's strategic position in the future. Right after that we have the company's investment and its ROI.

If the company's CCR is not overloaded, that is if the company's constraint is its ability to increase its sales, there will be no difference between the maximum profit mix and the marketing mix columns, because the company will not need to choose what to produce and sell, since it has enough capacity to deliver all the market's demand for its products.

The company needs to define the time period that it will use as a base for the data used in the statements; i.e., if it will do weekly, monthly or quarterly forecasts and simulations.

Capacity of CCR—Units of time (most commonly in minutes) that the CCR is available to process the company's products. Here it is very important to enter the real time the CCR is available, taking into account maintenance time, downtime and anything that decreases the availability of the CCR.

Demand/CCR Capacity—Here we divide the units of time on the CCR needed to produce all the demand by the CCR's capacity. If this number exceeds 100% it means that the plant does not have enough capacity to produce all the demand.

Product—Same name/code as the previous statement.

Demand—The nature of this variable will depend on the company's market and the time horizon chosen. If it is a company that works with customer orders and the period chosen for the analysis is not very long, this column can be filled with the customers' orders. If, on the other hand, the company works with sales forecasts for each product and/or the time horizon is long, this column should be filled with the sales forecast for each product. This quantity can be in product units, tons, etc. It is important that the unit used be the same in all the product measurements: price, TVC, time on CCR and demand.

Maximum Throughput Mix—This column gives the maximum throughput mix for the period being analyzed. This is done by taking into account the CCR's capacity, the products' demand, the products' time on the CCR and the products' profitabilities. The maximum throughput mix will be equal to the demand column until the accumulated utilization of the CCR reaches 100%. From this point downwards the maximum throughput mix will be zero for all products (these are the least profitable products). If the constraint is not the CCR (the company can sell more than its demand) then the maximum throughput mix will be equal to the demand.

Sales Mix—In most cases companies cannot impose a product mix on the market. What happens is that many products, even when they are not that profitable for the company, have to be sold to satisfy the market. Therefore, they must, using demand as a base, build a marketing mix. This column contains the quantity the company has decided to produce and sell of each product in the period being analyzed. If the company's CCR is idle, this column will be the same as the demand column and the maximum throughput mix column. But if the CCR is overloaded, this column will be different because each product quantity can only be equal to or less than the quantity in the demand column.

The following columns are all a consequence of the data of the previous columns. These columns are all divided into two parts. The first part shows the data for the maximum throughput mix (column I), and the second part shows the data for the company's sales mix (column J). When the CCR is not overloaded these two parts will be the same.

Accumulated Utilization of the CCR—In this column we keep track of the accumulated utilization of the CCR. We multiply the quantity to be produced of each product (column I or J) by the time each product uses of the CCR (column E) and divide this result by the CCR's availability. Then we just accumulate these percentages as we go down the statement. At the left part of the column, where we accumulate the utilization of the CCR to supply the maximum throughput mix, we can verify if the company's constraint is in its plant when the accumulated utilization of the CCR is equal to 100%. When the accumulated utilization is less than 100% this column shows us what percentage of the CCR's capacity is idle. The other side of this column accumulates the CCR's utilization to produce the sales mix. It cannot be greater than 100% because the company should not promise to deliver what it cannot produce.

Total Throughput per Product—This results from the multiplication of the maximum throughput mix quantity (column I) or the sales mix quantity (column J) by the Throughput per Unit (column D). It shows how much each product contributes to the company's total throughput.

Total Throughput of the Company—This is the total of all the products' throughput. It shows how much fresh money is going to be generated by the company. At the left side of this line we have the maximum throughput this company can generate in the period being analyzed. At the right side of this line we have the total throughput this company will generate based on the sales mix. This way we find the company's maximum throughput, and therefore, the maximum net profit it can generate under the given circumstances.

Net Profit—Difference between the company's Total Throughput and its Operating Expense.

Net Profit Difference—Difference between the net profit generated by the maximum profit mix and the sales mix. Shows how much net profit the company is sacrificing in the short-run to guarantee its long-run.

Investment—The value of all the firm's assets. Remember that there is no value added to the company's WIP and finished goods inventory; these are valued at the price paid for the raw material and parts purchased to make them. Here we have the same debates that we have in conventional accounting: What value should we use for the assets? Market value? Historical value? I am not going to debate the issues, but this does not stop us from measuring the impact our decisions have on the company's bottom line. We can only measure the variation of the company's throughput, investment and operating expense and, consequently, calculate the incremental NP and ROI. If the incremental ROI of the suggested proposal is greater than a previously established ROI, then the proposal should be accepted.

Return on Investment—This is the annualized net profit divided by the investment. It measures the rate at which the company's investment is being rewarded.

Up until now we have seen how to use these statements to classify the products in order of profitability, to calculate the maximum profit the company can generate in the given conditions and to forecast the financial results for a determined time period. Now we will see how to use these statements, with slight modifications, to supply the information needed to make managerial decisions.

Table 4-4
Simulation—Month xx
Capacity of CCR = Demand/CCR capacity =

G	H	I	J	K		L (I or J x D)	
Product	**Demand (Forecast)**	**Maximum Throughput Mix**	**Sales Mix**	**Acum. Utiliz. of CCR %**		**Total Throughput per Product**	
	0	0	0	0.0%	0.0%	0	0
	0	0	0	0.0%	0.0%	0	0
	0	0	0	0.0%	0.0%	0	0

Total Throughput 0 0
Variation in OE = 0 Operating Expense 0 0

Net Profit	0	0
(NP difference)	0	
NP difference between analyzed alternatives		0
Investment necessary		0
Proposal's ROI (annual)		0.0%
Investment	0	0
ROI (annual)	0.0%	0.0%

The only difference here is in the bottom part of the statement. Here we have a new field, where we can enter the forecasted variation of OE if we implement the suggestion being analyzed. Farther along we compare the difference between the NP of the current situation with the NP of the proposed suggestion. If this difference is positive the proposed suggestion increases the company's NP. But this might not be enough to increase the financial position of the company, depending on the investment needed. If there is any investment involved, we need to make sure that the additional investment is enough to compensate for it. To do that, on the next line we have a field to enter the additional investment, and right after that, we have calculated the ROI of this proposal, the division between the incremental NP and the extra investment needed to generate it. Then we have the company's total investment, which has already increased due to this additional investment. We can also compare the company's current ROI with its ROI after the proposal.

As I already mentioned, there is a lot of debate about how to evaluate the investment in the company. Even so, this does not impede us from being able to analyze suggestions for improvements in the company's bottom line, as we can do an incremental analysis of the results. Calculating the variation in throughput and in OE we can calculate the incremental NP that the proposal will generate. If this analyzed proposal does not need any investment, it need only increase the NP, and the company's profitability will increase. When the proposal demands an investment, we need to divide the incremental NP by the investment needed to generate it, calculating the proposal's ROI. Comparing this ROI with a previously established ROI, the company can verify if the proposal is worthwhile or not.

By utilizing these statements to make decisions, we are really trying to answer the three questions we posed in the previous chapter: What is the variation in throughput? What is the variation in investment? and What is the variation in OE? If we can answer these three questions, we will be able to know if the analyzed suggestion takes the company toward its goal or not.

These statements allow for forecasts and simulations. In a very short time managers can simulate some improvement suggestions, appropriation requests, clients' proposals and so on. The decision process becomes much more transparent and accessible. The fact that Throughput Accounting (TA) does not allocate the OE to the products is the reason for such flexibility, as well as the guarantee of high quality information.

4.2. Examples of the Use of the Throughput Accounting Statements

Now that we better understand these statements and how to create them, we must understand their usefulness. These statements provide information that help managers to make decisions. Alone, they are not sufficient for managers to make every decision because they only show the forecasted financial results for a previously established time period. The goal of a company is not to make money today, but to make money today and in the future. To guarantee the company's future we often have to reduce its profits in the present. Managers should use these statements to see the impact of an analyzed decision on the company's profitability. Following this stage managers can make their decisions, such as whether they will implement or not the improvements suggested in the production processes, in marketing strategies, in plant expansions, in buying new equipment.

These statements alone are not sufficient for managers to make decisions, but managers should not make decisions without them. Without such statements in hand, managers are making decisions without knowing their impact on the company's profitability.

Now let us use some examples to better understand the use of these statements, and see how simple and quick it is to make good decisions using TOC.

As an example, let us use the company Right-Time, which makes watches.

The company's OE is US$ 112,335, as shown on the statement below.

Table 4-5

Item	US$
Wages	68,523.03
Energy	2,345.75
Rent	8,935.67
Depreciation	7,851.32
Telephone	2,978.73
Publicity	6,464.26
Transport	4,766.68
Others	10,469.56
Total	**112,335.00**

The company has seven products, and the profitability ranking of these products is the following.

Table 4-6
Data Base of Products

Product	Price	TVC	Throughput per Unit (Tu)	Time on CCR (min)	Tu/Min on CCR
Lady	68	42	26	0	
Classic	120	35	85	5	**17.0**
Goldstar	343	134	209	15	**13.93**
Sportsman	254	71	183	15	**12.20**
Yacht	147	56	91	8	**11.38**
Kids	35	4	31	3	**10.33**
Champion	97	42	55	7	**7.86**

According to the ranking, the most profitable product for the company is Lady, which does not use any time on the CCR; after comes product Classic with a US$ 17 per minute of the CCR; and the least profitable product is Champion, with a US$ 7.86 per minute of the CCR.

Now let us examine some examples of how these statements can be used to help us make decisions. We will use two scenarios: In the first one the company's constraint is in its plant, it is its CCR; and in the second one the company's CCR is idle, that is, the market is not buying everything the company can produce.

4.2.1. Constraint on the CCR

In this first analysis we will assume that the market is overheated, that is, the constraint is the CCR, which is available 8 hours a day, 22 days a month. With a 95% efficiency, there are 10,032 minutes available per month.[47]

With these data we can now forecast next month's profit.

Table 4-7
Maximum Profit Mix / Sales Mix
Capacity of CCR = 10,032   Demand / CCR capacity = 111.5%

Product	Demand (Forecast)	Maximum Throughput Mix	Sales Mix	Acum. Utiliz. of CCR %		Total Throughput per Product	
Lady	660	660	660	0.0%	0.0%	17,160	17.160
Classic	420	420	420	20.9%	20.9%	35,700	35,700
Goldstar	110	110	110	37.4%	37.4%	22,990	22,990
Sportsman	250	250	250	74.8%	74.8%	45,750	45,750
Yacht	200	200	149	90.7%	86.6%	18,200	13,559
Kids	300	300	50	99.7%	88.1%	9,300	1,550
Champion	170	4	170	100%	100%	220	9,350

Total Throughput	149,320	146,059
Operating Expense[48]	112,335	112,335
Net Profit	36,985	33,724

48 Here, for simplicity's sake, we are going to assume that OE does not vary if we vary the production mix. When this is not true, you have to include the variation in OE in your analysis.

47 8 x 60 = 480 minutes a day. Minutes available a month = 480 x 22 = 10,560. 95% efficiency = 10,560 x 0.95 = 10,032 minutes a month.

(NP difference)	3,261		
Investment		2,100,000	2,100,000
ROI (annual)		21.1%	19.3%

The Demand/CCR capacity shows that the company would need 11.5% more capacity on the CCR to be able to deliver all the forecasted demand.

Since the company's constraint is in its plant (that is, it cannot produce everything the market wants), we must decide which products we are going to produce and which we are not going to produce. To calculate the maximum profit the company can generate in this situation, TOC classifies the products according to their Throughput/Time on CCR. In the above example the company would produce from product Lady to Champion. The accumulated utilization of the CCR is equal to 100% on product Champion, which means that we will not be able to produce all this product's demand. Of a demand of 170 units we will only be able to produce 4 units, as is shown on the column of maximum throughput mix.[49]

Thus, the maximum profit mix is: 660 Lady + 420 Classic + 110 Goldstar + 250 Sportsman + 200 Yacht + 300 Kids + 4 Champion. With this mix the company's throughput for this period is US$ 149,320 and its OE is US$ 112,335 which results in a NP of US$ 36,985. The investment in the company is US$ 2,100,000, and therefore the ROI is a little bit higher than 21% a year.[50]

In most cases the company cannot sell only the products of its own choosing; it also must take into account marketing issues in order to guarantee profit in the future. For marketing reasons the company we are analyzing needs to deliver all the demand of product Champion (the least profitable one). What the statement clearly shows us is that if we are going to produce Champion we have to decide what product not to produce to free the 1,162 minutes needed on the CCR to produce the extra 166 units of Champion. Here the company is obliged to decide what it will promise to the market. The statement does not allow the company to promise what

[49] Minutes used until product Kids = 10,000. Minutes available to produce product Champion = 10,032 - 10,000 = 32. Possible production of Champion = 32 minutes / 7 minutes per product 4.

[50] Annual Profit = US$ 36,985 x 12 = US$ 443,820. ROI = 443,820 / 2,100,000 21% a year.

it cannot deliver, something that the companies usually do when the demand is overheated. The fact that you promise more than you can deliver generates a great quantity of delayed orders (which in turn generate a lot of confusion and constant re-schedulings in the production) and, of course, dissatisfied customers.

No matter what product we will not produce, the NP will decrease, because we are trading one product for another with a lower Throughput/Time on CCR. In order to have the lowest possible impact on the NP we must choose the products that have the lowest Throughput/Time on CCR in the maximum profit mix. When defining the sales mix we have to take into account the short-run and the long-run. We have to take into account the Throughput/Time on CCR and the market segmentation, the customers' needs, and so on. The sales mix column shows the chosen mix for this company.

With this mix the accumulated utilization of the CCR is 100%. The mix now is: 660 Lady + 420 Classic + 110 Goldstar + 250 Sportsman + 149 Yacht + 50 Kids + 170 Champion. To supply all of Champion's demand we decided not to produce part of the demand for Yacht and Kids. With this mix, the company's throughput is US$ 146,059 (US$ 3,261 less), and its OE is US$ 112,335 (no change), which result in a NP of US$ 33,724. The investment did not change and the ROI therefore decreased; now it is a bit higher than 19% a year.

This scenario will be the basis for our analysis of some common decisions in the daily life of a company.

First Analysis—Increase the CCR's capacity with an increase in the OE.

The foreman responsible for the CCR brought an idea to be analyzed: Hire another worker to help the CCR's operator. By doing this, they would waste less time on the machine's setups, and could increase its efficiency from 95% to 97.5%, gaining another 264 minutes a month.[51] OE would increase US$ 600 a month.

Here we have the analysis for this idea.

[51] Increase in efficiency = 2.5%. Increase in the minutes available on the constraint = 2.5% x 10,560 minutes = 264 minutes.

Table 4-8
Financial Simulation
Capacity of CCR = 10,296 Demand /CCR capacity = 108.7%

Product	Demand (Forecast)	Maximum Throughput Mix	Sales Mix	Acum. Utiliz. of CCR %		Total Throughput per Product	
Lady	660	660	660	0.0%	0.0%	17,160	17.160
Classic	420	420	420	20.4%	20.4%	35,700	35,700
Goldstar	110	110	110	36.4%	36.4%	22,990	22,990
Sportsman	250	250	250	72.8%	72.8%	45,750	45,750
Yacht	200	200	182	88.4%	87.0%	18,200	16,562
Kids	300	300	50	97.1%	88.4%	9,300	1,550
Champion	170	42	170	100%	100%	2,310	9,350

Total Throughput 151,410 149,062
Variation in OE = 600 Operating Expense 112,935 112,935

Net Profit 38,475 36,127
(NP difference) 2,348

NP difference between
analyzed alternatives 2,403
Investment necessary 0

Investment 2,100,000 2,100,000
ROI (annual) 22% 20.6%

With this increase in the constraint's availability, we can now produce more products. Previously we delivered 149 units of Yachts and now we are able to deliver 182 units a month. This makes the company's total throughput increase to US$ 149,062, which with an OE of US$ 112,935 (already with the US$ 600 increase), generates a profit of US$ 36,127. This idea increases profit by US$ 2,403, and as there is no need for investments, the ROI increases from 19.3% to 20.6%. Thus, the idea should be accepted.

Even though accepting this idea makes a lot of sense, it would most likely never be approved in a company that uses cost accounting and its measurements of local efficiencies. The new worker's efficiency would not be very high and he would have a lot of idle time because he would only help in the setups of the CCR (and cost accounting does not even recognize the existence of a CCR). Later on we will see in more detail the basic differences between throughput accounting and cost accounting.

Second Analysis—Reduce prices for a customer in exchange for an increase in volume.

A client (a big department store) called the marketing department and demanded a 20% discount on Yacht. In return, the department store agreed to increase volume by 35%. If the company does not accept this proposal, the client will buy the product from another vendor. This client is the sole buyer of Yacht, which means that if we do not give the discount we will not sell the product at all.

To analyze this proposal we first need to quantify the impact of losing this client on the company's bottom line, and then compare it to the impact of giving the discount and increasing the volume.

In the following statement we quantify the loss of the client.

Table 4-9
Financial Simulation
Capacity of CCR = 10,032 Demand/CCR capacity = 95.6%

Product	Demand (Forecast)	Maximum Throughput Mix	Sales Mix	Acum. Utiliz. of CCR %		Total Throughput per Product	
Lady	660	660	660	0.0%	0.0%	17,160	17,160
Classic	420	420	420	20.9%	20.9%	35,700	35,700
Goldstar	110	110	110	37.4%	37.4%	22,990	22,990
Sportsman	250	250	250	74.8%	74.8%	45,750	45,750
Yacht	0	0	0	74.8%	74.8%	0	0
Kids	300	300	300	83.7%	83.7%	9,300	9,300
Champion	170	42	170	95.6%	95.6%	9,350	9,350

Total Throughput	140,250	140,250
Operating Expense	112,335	112,335
Net Profit	27,915	27,915
(NP difference) 0		
Investment	2,100,000	2,100,000
ROI (annual)	16%	16%

With the loss of this client the CCR is no longer overloaded, which allows the company to supply all the demand for the other products. With the loss of product Yacht the company loses US$ 13,559 in throughput, but can increase Kids' throughput by US$ 7,750, which adds up to a net loss of US$ 5,809. As the OE was not affected, the NP decreased US$ 5,809, giving a ROI of 16%.

Now let us quantify the acceptance of the client's proposal. To do this we have to rebuild the data base of the products, as we are changing the selling price of product Yacht.

Table 4-10
Data Base of Products

Product	Price	TVC	Throughput per Unit (Tu)	Time on CCR (min)	Tu/Min on CCR
Lady	68	42	26	0	
Classic	120	35	85	5	**17.0**
Goldstar	343	134	209	15	**13.93**
Sportsman	254	71	183	15	**12.20**
Kids	35	4	31	3	**10.33**
Champion	97	42	55	7	**7.86**
Yacht	118	56	62	8	**7.75**

Before the discount, product Yacht was the fifth most profitable product (of a total of seven). With the discount it is now the least profitable. This data are sufficient for us to know that the company's profit will decrease if we accept this proposal, because the CCR is still overloaded (as a matter of fact it is even more loaded now with the increase of 35% in Yacht's volume). Also, to deliver all Yacht's demand we will have to stop producing products that are more profitable. The question here is: Will the loss in profit be greater or smaller than the one caused by the loss of the client? The following statement shows the answer.

Table 4-11
Financial Simulation
Capacity of CCR = 10,032 Demand/CCR capacity = 117.1%

Product	Demand (Forecast)	Maximum Throughput Mix	Sales Mix	Acum. Utiliz. of CCR %		Total Throughput per Product	
Lady	660	660	660	0.0%	0.0%	17,160	17,160
Classic	420	420	420	20.9%	20.9%	35,700	35,700
Goldstar	110	110	110	37.4%	37.4%	22,990	22,990
Sportsman	250	250	185	74.8%	65.0%	45,750	33,855
Kids	300	300	51	83.7%	66.6%	9,300	1,581
Champion	170	170	170	95.6%	78.4%	9,350	9,350
Yacht	270	55	270	100%	100%	3,410	16,740

	Total Throughput		143,660	137,376
Variation in OE = 0	Operating Expense		112,335	112,335
	Net Profit		31,325	25,041
	(NP difference)	6,284		
	NP difference between analyzed alternatives			–2,874
	Investment necessary			0
	Investment		2,100,000	2,100,000
	ROI (annual)		17.9%	14.3%

The loss in throughput is greater if we accept the proposal; the difference in NP is US$ 2,874. The increase in volume does not compensate for the discount in price. These are the numbers the company has to make the decision, but the company also has to take into account the marketing aspects in order to decide whether or not to accept the proposal. What this new accounting has shown is that accepting the proposal will decrease the company's profitability in the period analyzed.

Third Analysis—Purchase of a more elaborate raw material, eliminating the need to process it internally.

Engineering, together with purchasing, wants to analyze the idea of buying a more elaborate raw material. This would eliminate the need for the company to process it because it would arrive ready to be assembled. This raw material is part of product Goldstar, and this extra processing by the vendor will cost the company US$ 10, increasing this product's TVC from US$ 134 to US$ 144. By using this the company will be able to reduce its OE by US$ 650. The following statements evaluate this idea:

We first need to rebuild the data base of the products, as Throughput per Unit of product Goldstar decreased.

Table 4-12
Data Base of Products

Product	**Price**	**TVC**	**Throughput per Unit (Tu)**	**Time on CCR (min)**	**Tu/Min on CCR**
Lady	68	42	26	0	
Classic	120	35	85	5	**17.00**
Goldstar	343	144	199	15	**13.27**
Sportsman	254	71	183	15	**12.20**
Yacht	147	56	91	8	**11.38**
Kids	35	4	31	3	**10.33**
Champion	97	42	55	7	**7.86**

Product Goldstar is still in the same place in the profitability ranking, even though its Tu/Time on CCR fell US$ 0.66. In the following statement we have the NP for this situation.

Table 4-13
Financial Simulation
Capacity of CCR = 10,032 Demand/CCR capacity = 111.5%

Product	Demand (Forecast)	Maximum Throughput Mix	Sales Mix	Acum. Utiliz. of CCR %		Total Throughput per Product	
Lady	660	660	660	0.0%	0.0%	17,160	17,160
Classic	420	420	420	20.9%	20.9%	35,700	35,700
Goldstar	110	110	110	37.4%	37.4%	21,890	21,890
Sportsman	250	250	250	74.8%	74.8%	45,750	45,750
Yacht	200	200	149	90.7%	86.6%	18,200	31,559
Kids	300	300	50	99.7%	88.1%	9,300	1,550
Champion	170	4	170	100%	100%	220	9,350

	Total Throughput	148,220	144,959
Variation in OE = – 650	Operating Expense	111,685	111,685
	Net Profit	36,535	33,274
	(NP difference)	3,261	
	NP difference between analyzed alternatives		–450
	Investment necessary		0
	Investment	2,100,000	2,100,000
	ROI (annual)	20.9%	19%

The NP fell US$ 450, which shows that the idea does not take the company towards its goal. This idea should not be implemented. The reduction in OE does not compensate the reduction in the company's throughput.

Fourth Analysis—Decrease a part's time on the CCR, making the vendor do part of the process.

The engineering and purchasing departments brought up another idea. They want to analyze an idea very similar to the last one, but this time the vendor's extra work will offload some work from the CCR. This raw material is part of Sportsman, and this extra process by the vendor will cost US$ 10, increasing this product's TVC from US$ 71 to US$ 81. In using this the company will be able to reduce this product's time on the CCR from 15 to 9 minutes. This procedure needs a US$ 15,000 investment in tools for the vendor, to be paid by Right-Time, which will also increase its OE (due to this investment's depreciation).

We first need to rebuild the data base of the products, as the Tu and time on CCR of product Sportsman both decreased.

Table 4-14
Data Base of Products

Product	**Price**	**TVC**	**Throughput per Unit (Tu)**	**Time on CCR (min)**	**Tu/Min on CCR**
Lady	68	42	26	0	
Sportsman	254	81	173	9	**19.22**
Classic	120	35	85	5	**17.00**
Goldstar	343	134	209	15	**13.93**
Yacht	147	56	91	8	**11.38**
Kids	35	4	31	3	**10.33**
Champion	97	42	55	7	**7.86**

The decrease in the time on CCR more than compensated the decrease in the product's throughput. Product Sportsman went from being fourth to second most profitable product. Let us see the impact this has on the company's profitability.

Table 4-15
Financial Simulation
Capacity of CCR = 10,032 Demand/CCR capacity = 96.6%

Product	Demand (Forecast)	Maximum Throughput Mix	Sales Mix	Acum. Utiliz. of CCR %		Total Throughput per Product	
Lady	660	660	660	0.0%	0.0%	17,160	17,160
Sportsman	250	250	250	22.4%	22.4%	43,250	43,250
Classic	420	420	420	43.4%	43.4%	35,700	35,700
Goldstar	110	110	110	59.8%	59.8%	22,990	22,990
Yacht	200	200	200	75.8%	75.8%	18,200	18,200
Kids	300	300	300	84.7%	84.7%	9,300	9,300
Champion	170	170	170	96.6%	96.6%	9,350	9,350

	Total Throughput	155,950	155,950
Variation in OE = 125	Operating Expense	12,460	112,460
	Net Profit	43,490	43,490
	(NP difference) 0		
	NP difference between analyzed alternatives		9,766
	Investment necessary		15,000
	Proposal's ROI (annual)		781.3%
	Investment	2,115,000	2,115,000
	ROI (annual)	24.7%	24.7%

This is a very good idea for the company. It increases the NP by US$ 9,766 with an investment of US$ 15,000, which generates a ROI of more than 781% a year! The company's total ROI goes from 19.3% to 24.7%. In addition, the CCR is no longer overloaded, so the company can deliver all the market's demand, leaving all its clients satisfied and creating room for more sales. As if this were not enough, the vendor also gained, as it will get US$ 10 more per part without making any investment and without increasing its OE. As a matter of fact the US$ 10 will go directly to its NP because the extra process it will do does not affect either its CCR or its OE, even though the vendor does not know that because he does not use TOC.

4.2.2. Constraint in the Market

We will use the same example of company Right-Time, but this time supposing its constraint is the market. This means that all its resources have enough capacity to supply what the market is demanding. Therefore, every product that has a selling price higher than its TVC contributes to the company's bottom line.

The data base of products does not change. What changes is the demand and the financial forecast.

Table 4-16
Maximum Profit Mix/Sales Mix
Capacity of CCR = 10,032 Demand/CCR capacity = 65%

Product	Demand (Forecast)	Maximum Throughput Mix	Sales Mix	Acum. Utiliz. of CCR %		Total Throughput per Product	
Lady	400	400	400	0.0%	0.0%	10,400	10,400
Classic	320	320	320	15.9%	15.9%	27,200	27,200
Goldstar	110	110	110	32.4%	32.4%	22,990	22,990
Sportsman	50	50	50	39.9%	39.9%	9,150	9,150
Yacht	90	90	90	47.0%	47.0%	8,190	8,190
Kids	250	250	250	54.5%	54.5%	7,750	7,750
Champion	150	150	150	65.0%	65.0%	8,250	8,250

Total Throughput		93,930	93,930
Operating Expense		112,335	112,335
Net Profit		–18,405	–18,405
(NP difference)	0		
Investment		2,100,000	2,100,000
ROI (annual)		–10.5%	–10.5%

The company's Total Throughput is US$ 93,930. Its OE is still US$ 112,335, which results in a loss of US$ 18,405. The CCR is being utilized 65% of its available time, which shows that the company has the capacity to produce more products; what it needs to do is to find the market for these products.

First Analysis—Export some products with lower prices than those used in the internal market.

As the constraint is the market, the marketing people want to evaluate the financial results of some strategies. The first one is to export two products, Classic and Sportsman, to South Korea. For these products to be accepted in this market the company must reduce their prices. Classic's price has to go from US$ 120 to US$ 72 and Sportsman's price has to go from US$ 254 to US$ 176. By doing this the data base of products shifts to the following.

Table 4-17
Data Base of Products

Product	**Price**	**TVC**	**Throughput per Unit (Tu)**	**Time on CCR (min)**	**Tu/Min on CCR**
Lady	68	42	26	0	
Classic	120	35	85	5	**17.00**
Goldstar	343	134	209	15	**13.93**
Sportsman	254	71	183	15	**12.20**
Yacht	147	56	91	8	**11.38**
Kids	35	4	31	3	**10.33**
Champion	97	42	55	7	**7.86**
Classic exp.	72	35	37	5	**7.40**
Sportsman exp.	176	71	105	15	**7.00**

Products Classic and Sportsman appear twice in this statement, as they have two different clients that pay two different prices. The products that are exported are the last ones on the list, that is, they are the least profitable ones when the company has an internal constraint. But, as their throughput per unit is positive and the company has excess capacity, they will certainly improve the company's bottom line. The demand in South Korea is 250 units for Classic exp. and 100 units for Sportsman exp. Let us see how much the firm's performance will improve.

Table 4-18
Financial Simulation
Capacity of CCR = 10,032 Demand/CCR capacity = 92.4%

Product	Demand (Forecast)	Maximum Throughput Mix	Sales Mix	Acum. Utiliz. of CCR %		Total Throughput per Product	
Lady	400	400	400	0.0%	0.0%	10,400	10,400
Classic	320	320	320	15.9%	15.9%	27,200	27,200
Goldstar	110	110	110	32.4%	32.4%	22,990	22,990
Sportsman	50	50	50	39.9%	39.9%	9,150	9,150
Yacht	90	90	90	47.0%	47.0%	8,190	8,190
Kids	250	250	250	54.5%	54.5%	7,750	7,750
Champion	150	150	150	65.0%	65.0%	8,250	8,250
Classic exp.	250	250	250	77.5%	77.5%	9,250	9,250
Sportsman exp.	100	100	100	92.4%	92.4%	10,500	10,500

	Total Throughput	113,680	113,680
Variation in OE = 250	Operating Expense	112,585	12,585
	Net Profit	1,095	1,095
	(NP difference) 0		
	NP difference between analyzed alternatives		19,500
	Investment necessary		0
	Investment	2,100,000	2,100,000
	ROI (annual)	0.6%	0.6%

As we can see the company also forecasted an increase of US$ 250 a month in its OE. With the increase in OE and the big discounts on the products, the company's loss turns into a profit of US$ 1,095. Clearly this strategy helps the company to move towards its goal. In a situation like this the company has to check that the prices used in the international market will not interfere with the prices in the internal market, or else the loss can become even worse.

The CCR is still idle, but its utilization is near 100%. This serves as a warning to the company that there is not much excess capacity left to try and increase profits by increasing volumes.

This means that if the internal market grows and if the company wants to increase its profits, it will have to stop selling, at least in part, to South Korea. This is important to point out because if the company signs a long-term contract with the South Koreans to supply the above quantities, it might be jeopardizing its future profits. It might be worthwhile to continue selling to South Korea in smaller quantities, when the internal market grows, in order to free capacity to sell the more profitable products. It might not be strategically worthwhile to stop selling completely to South Korea if the internal market grows, because in the event of a market downturn the company would not be able to turn to this external client. Here we have another example of how the company has to decide how much profit it will sacrifice in the short-term to guarantee its long-term.

This kind of strategy has been used many times (and still is) by the Japanese. Japanese electronic goods are much cheaper in America than in Japan. When the Japanese enacted this strategy, many people argued they were dumping, but time showed that they were not. According to the new concept of a company we are seeing in this book, the concept of dumping changes. Traditionally dumping occurs when a company sells a product below its production costs. As we have seen until now, the production cost of a product is not relevant because the costs belong to the company, not to the products. The only cost that is really a product cost is the TVC, which generally is the raw material cost. This means that dumping actually occurs when a company sells a product below its TVC, because only then will the company be losing money with the product. This changes the accusations of dumping a lot because the TVC are a small part of the company's costs, and its proportion is continuously decreasing, year by year.

Second Analysis—Reduce prices for a customer in exchange for an increase in volume.

This proposal is the same as proposal two in the previous scenario (when the company's constraint was its CCR). A client (a big department store) called the marketing department and demanded a 20% discount on Yacht. In return the department store agreed to increase volume by 35%. If the company does not accept this proposal, the client will buy the product from another vendor. This client is the sole buyer of Yacht, which means that if we do not give the discount we will not sell the product at all.

To analyze this proposal we first need to quantify the impact of losing this client on the company's bottom line, and then compare it to the impact of giving the discount and increasing the volume.

Table 4-19
Financial Simulation
Capacity of CCR = 10,032 Demand/CCR capacity = 57.8%

Product	Demand (Forecast)	Maximum Throughput Mix	Sales Mix	Acum. Utiliz. of CCR %		Total Throughput per Product	
Lady	400	400	400	0.0%	0.0%	10,000	10,400
Classic	320	320	320	15.9%	15.9%	27,200	27,200
Goldstar	110	110	110	32.4%	32.4%	22,990	22,990
Sportsman	50	50	50	39.9%	39.9%	9,150	9,150
Yacht	0	0	0	39.9%	39.9%	0	0
Kids	250	250	250	47.3%	47.3%	7,750	7,750
Champion	150	150	150	57.8%	57.8%	8,250	8,250

Total Throughput		85,740	85,740
Operating Expense		112,335	112,335
Net Profit		–26,595	–26,595
(NP difference)	0		
Investment		2,100,000	2,100,000
ROI (annual)		–15.2%	–15.2%

If the company loses the client its loss will be US$ 26,595. Let us see what happens if the proposal is accepted.

Table 4-20
Data Base of Products

Product	Price	TVC	Throughput per Unit (Tu)	Time on CCR (min)	Tu/Min on CCR
Lady	68	42	26	0	
Classic	120	35	85	5	**17.00**
Goldstar	343	134	209	15	**13.93**
Sportsman	254	71	183	15	**12.20**
Kids	35	4	31	3	**10.33**
Champion	97	42	55	7	**7.86**
Yacht	118	56	62	8	**7.75**

Product Yacht will be last in the profitability rank. Let us see if the acceptance of this order will worsen the company's performance.

Table 4-21
Financial Simulation
Capacity of CCR = 10,032 Demand/CCR capacity = 67.5%

Product	Demand (Forecast)	Maximum Throughput Mix	Sales Mix	Acum. Utiliz. of CCR %		Total Throughput per Product	
Lady	400	400	400	0.0%	0.0%	10,400	10,400
Classic	320	320	320	15.9%	15.9%	27,200	27,200
Goldstar	110	110	110	32.4%	32.4%	22,990	22,990
Sportsman	50	50	50	39.9%	39.9%	9,150	9,150
Kids	250	250	250	47.3%	47.3%	7,750	7,750
Champion	150	150	150	57.8%	57.8%	8,250	8,250
Yacht	122	122	122	67.5%	67.5%	7,564	7,564

	Total Throughput	93,304	93,304
Variation in OE = 0	Operating Expense	112,335	112,335

Net Profit	19,031	–19,031
(NP difference)		0
NP difference between analyzed alternatives		7,564
Investment necessary		0
Investment	2,100,000	2,100,000
ROI (annual)	–10.9%	–10.9%

If we accept the order the loss will be US$ 7,564 less than if we lose the client. Moreover, the loss hardly changes if we accept the order. In this case it is clearly better financially for the company to accept the proposal, which is the opposite of what we concluded for the same proposal when the constraint was the CCR. That is precisely why it is better to give the discount now, because the CCR is idle and the company will not be able to use the time that will be freed up on the CCR to produce other, more profitable products.

Third Analysis—Pruning of a product.

Since the company is losing money it wants to analyze the pruning Lady, because it has the lowest throughput per unit of all products. With this pruning the OE will be decreased by US$ 350 a month.

Table 4-22
Financial Simulation
Capacity of CCR = 10,032 Demand/CCR capacity = 65%

Product	Demand (Forecast)	Maximum Throughput Mix	Sales Mix	Acum. Utiliz. of CCR %		Total Throughput per Product	
Classic	320	320	320	15.9%	15.9%	27,200	27,200
Goldstar	110	110	110	32.4%	32.4%	22,990	22,990
Sportsman	50	50	50	39.9%	39.9%	9,150	9,150
Yacht	90	90	90	47.0%	47.0%	8,190	8,190
Kids	250	250	250	54.5%	54.5%	7,750	7,750
Champion	150	150	150	65.0%	65.0%	8,250	8,250

	Total Throughput	83,530	83,530
Variation in OE = –350	Operating Expense	111,985	111,985
	Net Profit	–28,455	–28,455
	(NP difference)	0	
	NP difference between analyzed alternatives		10,050
	Investment necessary		0
	Investment	2,100,000	2,100,000
	ROI (annual)	–16.3%	–16.3%

The pruning of some products is an alternative often considered. In this case we need to quantify the impact this pruning will have on the three measurements, as we did in the preceding statement. If we stop producing product Lady we will lose its throughput of US$ 10,400 a month. For this product's pruning to be financially worthwhile we must reduce the company's OE by more than US$ 10,400 a month. As the reduction was only US$ 350 a month, the loss increased by US$ 10,050. Therefore the company should maintain the product in its mix.

For the pruning of a product to increase the company's profitability, the reduction in OE must be greater than the loss in throughput. Therefore, in most cases, pruning of products is not financially advisable, because most of the company's resources are used by many products, which makes it impossible to have great reductions in OE when pruning a product.

4.3. Corporations

Now let us examine a case that generates a lot of doubts, even in companies that use TOC. How should a big corporation, with many different plants, evaluate its divisions' performance, and what treatment should be given to the OE of the headquarters?

We want to have a management information system that shows us what actions take us closer to the company's goal and which ones do not. We want to avoid local optimizations that jeopardize the global optimum.

What should we do with the headquarters OE? Should we allocate them to the plants according to a previously established variable?

We should not try to allocate the headquarters OE because this would generate some distortions. To make these allocations we would have to find a quantifiable variable that we could use to decide what part of the headquarters OE would go to each plant. This is similar to the allocations of a plant's OE to its products, and it generates the same distortions. Whatever the chosen parameter, the assumption behind this process is that if a plant increases this parameter then it will be increasing the headquarters OE, and this does not make much sense.

We have to keep in mind that the objective of an information system is to show who is contributing to the goal of the company. To evaluate the system's overall performance there is no problem. The problems arise when we want to evaluate the performance of a part of the system, of one specific plant.

The goal is to make money now as well as in the future. Therefore, we have to know if the plant is making money or not. Consequently, we should evaluate whether the money generated by this sub-system (plant) is greater than the money we spend to keep it working. We have to verify if this sub-system is bringing in fresh money to the system. In other words, we have to see if its throughput is greater than its OE: We have to calculate its Net Throughput (NT). This OE is the plant's specific OE, the only OE over which the plant has control.

With this we have an overall view of how much fresh money each plant is bringing into the corporation, and when adding these values we will get the corporation's total throughput. From this value we should subtract the headquarters OE to find the NP of the whole corporation.

Let us see an example of how to do this. In this example the corporation has three plants, each one selling to a different market. The first one, CompuCar, produces electronic equipment for cars; the second one, ElectroHome, produces household appliances; and the third one, GoodSound, produces stereos. As we have already seen enough through the use of the TA statements, we will not analyze here the individual performance of each company. Rather we will only see the relationship between them and the corporation.

CompuCar

Table 4-23
Operating Expense—August

Item	US$
Wages	134,256
Energy	7,654
Rent	22,371
Depreciation	24,563
Interest	4,374
Publicity	11,298
Transport	12,567
Others	29,871
Total	**246,954**

Table 4-24
Data Base of Products—August

Product	Price	TVC	Throughput per Unit (Tu)	Time on CCR (min)	Tu/Min on CCR
GL1	124	42	82	7	**11.71**
GL2	103	39	64	7	**9.14**
LX1	82	37	45	5	**9.00**
LS1	66	26	40	4.5	**8.89**
GL3	96	37	59	7	**8.43**
LX2	73	33	40	5	**8.00**
Stand 1	53	26	27	4.5	**6.00**
Stand 2	46	24	22	4.5	**4.89**

Product GL1 is the most profitable one, with a Tu/minute on CCR of US$ 11.71. The least profitable one is Stand2, with a Tu/minute on CCR of US$ 4.89. All the products go through the CCR, which, as the statement below shows, is the company's constraint.

Table 4-25
Financial Results—August
Capacity of CCR = 45,000 Demand/CCR capacity = 177.2%

Product	Demand (Forecast)	Maximum Throughput Mix	Sales Mix	Acum. Utiliz. of CCR %		Total Throughput per Product	
GL1	500	500	370	7.8%	5.8%	41,000	30,340
GL2	1,000	1,000	700	23.3%	16.6%	64,000	44,800
LX1	1,500	1,500	750	40.0%	25.0%	67,500	33,750
LS1	1,500	1,500	500	55.0%	30.0%	60,000	20,000
GL3	1,000	1,000	350	70.6%	35.4%	59,000	20,650
LX2	1,500	1,500	500	87.2%	41.0%	60,000	20,000
Stand 1	3,500	1,277	2,300	100%	64.0%	34,479	62,100
Stand 2	5,500	0	3,600	100%	100%	0	79,200

Total Throughput	385,979	310,840
Operating Expense	246,954	246,954
Net Throughput	139,025	63,886
(NT difference)	75,139	
Investment	5,000,000	5,000,000
ROI (annual)	33.4%	15.3%

The company generates a throughput of US$ 310,840, and has an OE of US$ 246,954, which results in a NT of US$ 63,886. Since the investment in this company is US$ 5,000,000, the ROI is 15.3%.

ElectroHome

Table 4-26
Operating Expense—August

Item	US$
Wages	435,211
Energy	15,342
Rent	56,789
Depreciation	27,690
Telephone	2,367
Publicity	55,476
Transport	85,294
Others	46,872
Total	**725,041**

Table 4-27
Data Base of Products—August

Product	Price	TVC	Throughput per Unit (Tu)	Time on CCR (min)	Tu /Min on CCR
Freezer LX	977	357	620	19	**32.63**
Freezer LS	853	331	522	19	**27.47**
AirCond LX	1,022	565	457	25	**18.28**
Stove 6m	345	209	136	13	**10.46**
Freezer st	213	121	92	14	**6.57**
Air Cond st	163	97	66	17	**3.88**
Stove 4m	111	75	36	13	**2.77**

This company's most profitable product is Freezer LX, with a Tu/minute on CCR of US$ 32.63. The least profitable one is Stove

4m, with a Tu/minute on CCR of US$ 2.77. All the products use the CCR, and as the statement below shows, this is the company's constraint.

Table 4-28
Financial Results—August
Capacity of CCR = 75,000   Demand/CCR capacity = 139.3%

Product	Demand (Forecast)	Maximum Throughput Mix	Sales Mix	Acum. Utiliz. of CCR %		Total Throughput per Product	
Freezer LX	200	200	200	5.1%	5.1%	124,000	124,000
Freezer LS	300	300	300	12.7%	12.7%	156,600	156,600
AirCondLX	800	800	674	39.3%	35.1%	365,600	308,018
Stove 6m	750	750	600	52.3%	45.5%	102,000	81,600
Freezer st	1,200	1,200	775	74.7%	60.0%	110,400	71,300
Air Cond st	1,700	1,114	1,000	100%	82.7%	73,524	66,000
Stove 4m	1,500	0	1,000	100%	100%	0	36,000

Total Throughput	932,124	843,518
Operating Expense	725,041	725,041
Net Throughput	207,083	118,477
(NT difference)	88,606	
Investment	8,000,000	8,000,000
ROI (annual)	31.1%	17.8%

The company generates a throughput of US$ 843,518, and has an OE of US$ 725,041, which result in a NT of US$ 118,477. Since the investment in this company is US$ 8,000,000, it generates a ROI of 17.8%.

GoodSound

Table 4-29
Operating Expense—August

Item	US$
Wages	795,872
Energy	35,648
Rent	25,468
Depreciation	89,631
Interest	12,367
Publicity	171,345
Transport	69,021
Others	46,872
Total	**1,246,224**

Table 4-30
Data Base of Products—August

Product	Price	TVC	Throughput per Unit (Tu)	Time on CCR (min)	Tu/Min on CCR
Blast Sp	256	98	158	9	**17.56**
Panel Lx	433	152	281	21	**13.38**
Eagle III	170	78	92	7	**13.14**
Eagle II	109	65	44	7	**6.29**
CD 5+1	145	76	69	11	**6.27**
Panel Ss	214	104	110	18	**6.11**
Walkman	35	20	15	2.5	**6.00**
Eagle I	59	42	17	3	**5.67**
Btast Std	115	74	41	8	**5.13**

Table 4-31
Financial Results—August
Capacity of CCR = 145,000 Demand/CCR capacity = 134.4%

Product	Demand	Maximum Throughput Mix	Sales Mix	Acum. Utiliz. of CCR %		Total Throughput per Product	
Blast Sp	1,100	1,100	1,100	6.8%	6.8%	173,800	173,800
Panel Lx	850	850	800	19.1%	18.4%	238,850	224,800
Eagle III	4,200	4,200	4,200	39.4%	38.7%	386,400	386,400
Eagle II	6,000	6,000	6,000	68.4%	67.7%	264,000	264,000
CD 5+1	570	570	250	72.7%	69.6%	39,330	17,250
Panel Ss	1,700	1,700	1,130	93.8%	83.6%	187,000	124,300
Walkman	1,600	1,600	500	96.6%	84.4%	24,000	7,500
Eagle I	12,400	1,660	6,000	100%	96.9%	28,220	102,000
Blast Std	2,200	0	570	100%	100%	0	23,370

Total Throughput	1,341,600	1,323,420
Operating Expense	1,246,224	1,246,224
Net Throughput	95,376	77,196
(NT difference)	18,180	
Investment	4,300,000	4,300,000
ROI (annual)	26.6%	21.5%

The company generates a throughput of US$ 1,323,420, and has an OE of US$ 1,246,224, resulting in a NT of US$ 77,196. Since the investment in this company is US$ 4,300,000, it generates a ROI of 21.5%.

Now let us see a way of consolidating these results in one statement for all the plants.

Consolidated

Table 4-32
Operating Expense Headquarters—August

Item	US$
Wages	98,569
Energy	3,928
Depreciation	14,856
Interest	3,256
Publicity	2,590
Transport	12,744
Others	29,874
Total	**165,817**

Table 4-33
Consolidated Financial Results—August

Unit	Throughput	% Total	Oper. Exp.	Net Throughput	% Total	Invest.	%	ROI
CompuCar	310,840	12.5%	246,954	63,886	24.6%	5,000,000	28.9%	15.3%
ElectroHome	843,518	34%	725,041	118,477	45.6%	8,000,000	46.2%	17.8%
GoodSound	1,323,420	53.4%	1,246,224	77,196	29.7%	4,300,000	24.9%	21.5%
Total	2,477,778	100%	2,218,219	**259,559**	100%	17,300,000	100%	

Headquarter OE	165,817
NP corporation	**93,742**
Headquarter Investment	250,000
Total Investment	17,550,000
ROI	**6.4%**

The total of the plants' net throughput is equal to US$ 259,559. This is the amount that the three plants together contribute to the corporation's profits. To calculate the NP of the corporation we need to subtract the headquarters OE from this amount.[52] Thus, the total NP is U$ 93,742, and since the total investment is US$ 17,550,000, the ROI is 6.4% a year.

By using the above statement we can evaluate the individual performance of the plants. GoodSound is the one with the best performance, with 53.4% of the corporation's total throughput, 29.7% of the total NT and 24.9% of the total investment, which results in the best ROI of all—21.5%. But ElectroHome is the one with the worst performance: It has 45.6% of the total NT and 46.2% of the total investment, which results in the worst ROI of all—17.8%.

The performance of the three plants is good, but cannot be compared directly with the performance of a plant that is not part of a corporation because an independent plant has additional expenses that corporate units do not have. Most likely each one of them do not have a complete accounting department, a purchasing department and so on, because headquarters often performs these functions. This is one of the advantages of being part of a corporation; many common things can be shared, and a synergy can be created. Without these factors, the existence of a headquarters OE does not make much sense. This OE should also be measured, in order to gauge whether having such a headquarters brings any benefits.

There is still another question I would like to answer. How do we know if a plant is contributing to the profitability of the corporation? Very simply, we should use the same method we used to decide whether it is worthwhile to prune a product: We calculate if the system's profitability will increase without the plant in question. To make closing a plant worthwhile the decrease in headquarters OE and total investment must compensate for the loss of the plant's net throughput. By doing so the corporation's ROI will increase.

In most cases, the closing of a single plant does not imply a great reduction in headquarters OE because the headquarters resources are used by many plants, which makes it difficult to decrease a lot of OE when closing one plant. The larger the corporation, with more plants, the greater the intensity of this phenomena.

[52] If the headquarters generates any throughput, this amount should be added to this calculation.

4.4. Conclusion

TA statements are simple, easy to implement and extremely useful, as long as the company can make the transition from the cost world to the throughput world. This methodology can only be fully exploited when the company is imbued with the "throughput world" philosophy.

TOC's accounting is **simple** and **logical;** consequently, it is **understood by all.** Not only that, it supplies **trustworthy information fast,** which allows managers to **make good decisions fast.** These are the qualities a management information system should have, and which no other system currently offers.

Now that you have seen TOC's basic concepts and how to use its accounting statements, you can build these statements for your company. But, beware of the surprises! Some products that you thought were very profitable will show up as not so profitable, and other products, that you thought were not very profitable, will show up as very profitable. But the biggest surprise will be when you realize how much you can increase your profit simply by changing your sales mix (this will only happen if your CCR is overloaded), and when you realize that the majority of the improvements projects and the appropriations requests your company approved, based on cost accounting information, in fact hurt the company's profitability.[53] (We will see this in the following chapters.)

Let us return for a moment to the answer to the second question that we saw at the end of chapter 2: Do we need to allocate costs to products? In other words, do we need product costs to make decisions? We made various decisions without allocating any costs to products. In fact, we can make any decision without using costs (we will see some other types of decisions in other chapters). Therefore, we can conclude that, even if costing can supply good information, we do not need to use it because throughput accounting also supplies good information, with a simpler and more agile method.

However, this brings us to the first question at the end of chapter 2: Can we still change cost methods so that they can give us good information? The following chapters will answer this question.

[53] This will also bring up these questions. For how long have you been missing these opportunities? How much is cost accounting costing you?

5
Throughput Accounting v. Cost Accounting

Management accounting is turning out not to be capable of providing managers with information necessary to make good decisions. There are many debates about what functions a management accounting system should have, and consequently, what information is necessary to make decisions.

In this book we are analyzing management accounting's function of making connections between the local actions/decisions of managers and the company's profitability, so that the managers can judge what actions/decisions take the company towards its goal.

Therefore, we need information that tells us if the decision being analyzed increases the company's profitability. From this point of view, we are going to analyze which alternative—cost accounting or throughput accounting—better fulfills this goal. In chapter 2 we saw an example in which cost accounting did not provide the correct information. In the next example we will compare the information provided by cost accounting with the one provided by throughput accounting, making clear their differences.

When I say cost accounting I mean traditional costing, Activity-Base Costing (ABC), Strategic Cost Management and any other methodology that uses cost as a base. All these methodologies share the same basic assumptions; they are all part of the same paradigm (as we will see in chapter 9). We will use ABC to make the comparison between the two (TOC and cost accounting).

ABC uses activity analysis and product cost to verify if the decision increases the company's profitability. Throughput accounting, on the other hand, uses the impact on its three measurements (throughput, investment and operating expense) to answer the same question.

To be able to compare these two approaches we will use an example. In this example all external influences on the company have been eliminated, so we can really compare just the decision process. The prices are fixed, the market demand does not change, the machines do not break down, quality is perfect, there is no absenteeism, and vendors deliver everything you order on time.

5.1. Example

Figure 5-1
Process Flow

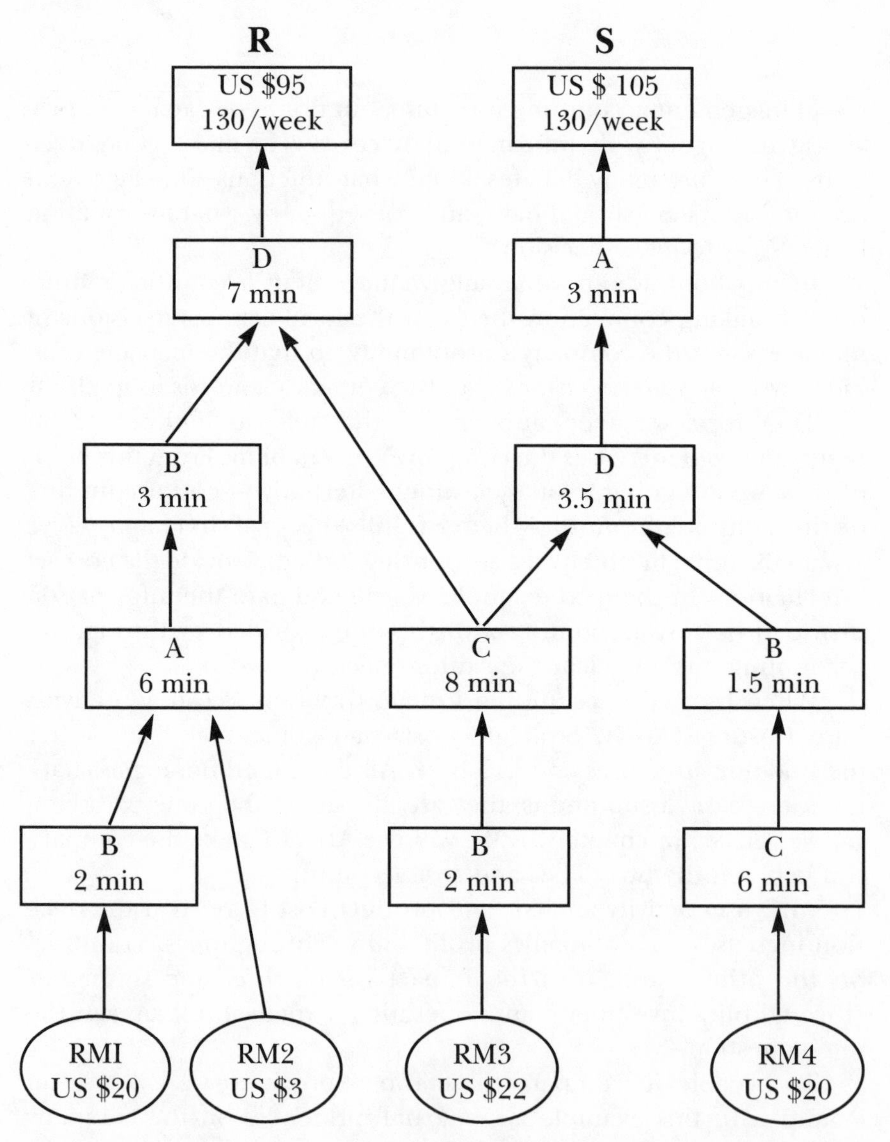

This diagram is not the layout, but the process flow. The company has four different resources, A, B, C and D, one unit of each. It sells two products, R and S. Product R is sold at US $95 a unit, and has a weekly demand of 130 units. Product S is sold at US $105 a unit, and its weekly demand is also 130 units.

Product R is comprised of three raw materials, RM1, RM2 and RM3. Let us assume RM1 as an example. It is processed first on resource B for 2 minutes, then it is assembled on resource A with RM2 in 6 minutes. They then go to resource B where they are processed for 3 minutes and they are finally assembled with RM3 on resource D, in 7 minutes.

Product R has a raw material cost of US$ 45. Product S uses only two raw materials, RM3 and RM4. Its raw material costs are US$ 42. As we can see, both products use RM3.

Each resource has one worker, and they all work 8 hours a day, 5 days a week, which results in an availability of 2,400 minutes a week per resource. The operating expenses are US$ 12,000 (which include rent, energy, direct labor, wages), in short, everything the company spends to keep itself running.

We already have the scenario for the example. Now, we are going to use ABC and TA to determine which product mix maximizes the company's profitability.

Our instinct would be to calculate what the profit would be if we sold all the demand for both products. However, the company does not have the capacity to produce 130 R and 130 S in a week because resource C does not have enough capacity (see the following table).

Table 5-1

Resource	**Minutes necessary for R**	**Minutes necessary for S**	**Total necessary minutes**	**Necessary minutes/available minutes**
A	780	390	1,170	48.8%
B	910	455	1,365	56.9%
C	**1,040**	**1,820**	**2,860**	**119.2%**
D	910	455	1,365	56.9%

In this case, to maximize the company's profitability, we need to know which product is the most profitable one, and then sell all of its demand and only then, if there is time left on resource C, sell the other product.

Let us now see how ABC and TOC resolve this matter.

5.1.1. ABC's Solution

ABC needs to calculate the products' costs in order to inform which product is most profitable. To do this ABC proposes the allocation of all the company's costs using many allocation bases, and by doing so presumes that the problem of lost relevance is resolved. Because ABC uses various cost drivers, costs are grouped in smaller cells and, according to ABC's supporters, this provides better information about the variation in costs. ABC also uses cost drivers that are not directly related to production volume.

> Conventional cost systems focus on the product in the costing process. Costs are traced to the product because each product item is assumed to consume the resources. Conventional allocation bases thus measure only attributes of the individual product item: the number of direct labor hours or material dollars consumed. By contrast, activities are the focus of the costing process in activity-based cost systems. Costs are traced from activities to products based on the product's demand for these activities during the production process. The allocation bases used in activity-based costing are thus measures of the activities performed.[54]

In ABC the cost of a product results from its consumption of the activities needed to produce and sell it. Therefore, we need to figure out which activities are used by the products, how much of these activities each product use and how much these activities cost. To be able to identify the use of the resources by the activities and the use of the activities by the products, we need to establish the factors that determine these uses.

To analyze company RS, we will use a simplified ABC model.[55] We need to identify the company's activities, their costs, their cost

[54] COOPER, Robin. "The Rise of Activity-Based Costing—Part One: What Is an Activity-Based Cost System?" *Journal Of Cost Management for the Manufacturing Industry,* Summer 1988, p. 45.

[55] For more details on activity-based costing see the bibliography at the end of this book.

drivers and the cost drivers' capacities. This company has identified three activities to trace the costs to the products.

The following table shows the company's activities and their cost.

Table 5-2
Total Cost of the Activities

Activity	US$
Production	$4,730
Quality Testing	$3,024
Shipping	$4,246
Total	**$12,000**

Now that we already have the cost of the three activities, we need to trace them to the products. In order to do this, we have to identify the cost driver rate. The cost driver rate is the activity cost divided by the cost driver capacity. Table 5-3 calculates the cost driver rate for our three activities.

Table 5-3
Cost Driver Rates

Activity	Activity Cost	Cost Driver	Cost Driver Capacity	Cost Driver Rate
Production	4,730	Resource hours	160	29.5625
Quality Testing	3,024	Hours of test time	40	75.60
Shipping	4,246	Pounds	4,000	1.0615

For the production activity the cost driver is the products' use of the production resources.

Table 5-4
Use of the Resources by the Products (Minutes)

	R	S
A	6	3
B	7	3.5
C	8	14
D	7	3.5
Total	**28**	**24**

From this we can trace the cost of the production activity to the products.

Table 5-5
Tracing Production Costs to Products

	R	S
Resource Hours	0.467	0.4
Cost Driver Rate	29.5625	29.5625
Production cost/unit	13.81	11.83

For the quality testing activity the cost driver is the hours of test time.

Table 5-6
Tracing Quality Test Time Costs to Products

	R	S
Test Time (Hours)	0.13	0.20
Cost Driver Rate	75.60	75.60
Quality Test Cost/Unit	9.83	15.12

For the shipping activity the cost driver is pounds.

Table 5-7
Tracing Quality Test Time Costs to Products

	R	S
Pounds	10	2
Cost Driver Rate	1.0615	1.0615
Shipping cost/unit	10.62	2.12

Now that we already have traced the costs of the three activities to the two products we can calculate the total cost per unit.

Table 5-8
Total Costs per Unit

	R	S
Direct Materials	45	42
Production	13.81	11.83
Quality Testing	9.83	15.12
Shipping	10.62	2.12
Total	**79.26**	**71.07**

Product R absorbs the greater part of the costs because the cost drivers showed that this product uses more the company's activities than product S.

If product R has lower price, higher cost of raw material and higher activity costs, we can only conclude that it is the least profitable product. Thus, to maximize the company's profitability we should give preference to product S, and then, if there is any time left on resource C, we should produce product R. We will produce all the S the market wants to buy (130 units). Producing this quantity will still leave 580 minutes available on resource C, which allows for the production of 72 units of R. Therefore, according to this methodology, the maximum profit mix is: 130 S + 72 R. Table 5-9 shows this mix's profit.

Table 5-9
RS's Maximum Profit According to ABC

	R	S	Total
Revenues	6,840	13,650	20,490
Raw Material Cost	3,240	5,460	8,700
Gross Margin	3,600	8,190	11,790
Operating Expense			12,000
Maximum Profit			**–210**

According to ABC's analysis, this company cannot generate profit in the current situation.

To stop losing money, the company will stop producing and selling product R. Apart from that, the marketing director was able to increase product S's demand up to the CCR's capacity limits, which is 171 units. Thus, the company will only sell product S. Let us calculate the impact this will have on the company's profitability.

Table 5-10
RS's Profit with the New Mix

	S
Revenues	17,955
Raw Material Cost	7,182
Gross Margin	10,773
Operating Expense	12,000
Net Profit	–1,227

The end result does not make much sense. We increased the sales of the most profitable product and we pruned the product that was losing money, and the company's loss increased! Try to explain that to the marketing manager!

5.1.2. TA's Solution

To do the TOC analysis we need some of the data we already saw in the previous analysis and some other data not considered by ABC. We need each product's throughput and each product's throughput/time of CCR.

Table 5-11
Data Base of Products

Product	Price	TVC	Throughput per Unit (Tu)	Time on CCR	Throughput /Time on CCR
R	95	45	50	8	6.25
S	105	42	63	14	4.5

With the throughput/time on the CCR, we can see that product R is the product that most contributes to the company's profitability. This is a completely different prioritization than ABC.

To calculate the maximum profit using this approach, we need to establish the sales mix. We will produce and sell all the Rs the market wants (130 units). In doing so there will still be 1,360 minutes available on the CCR, which we will use to produce 97 units of S. Therefore, according to TOC, the maximum profit mix is: 130R + 97 S.

Table 5-12
Maximum Profit According to TOC

Product	Mix	Acum. Utiliz. of CCR%	Total Throughput per Product
R	130	43.3%	6,500
S	97	100%	6,111

Total Throughput	12,611
Oper. Exp.	12,000
Net Profit	**611**

TOC's approach shows that the company, even by not changing anything about its current situation, can generate a profit of US$ 611 a week. And we were about to close this plant down!

The same marketing manager was able to increase product R's sales up to the CCR's capacity limits, which is 300 units. Let us see the impact on profit.

Table 5-13
Profit with New Sales Mix

Product	Sales Mix	Acum. Utiliz. of CCR%	Total Throughput per Product
R	300	100%	15,000

Total Throughput	15,000
Oper. Exp.	12,000
Net Profit	**3,000**

Now it makes more sense. When we increase the sales of the product that the approach says is more profitable, the profits really increase, which is the least we should expect of an information system!

5.2. Conclusion

The company is the same; what changed was the way we treated the available data. ABC needs to trace all the costs to the products, and this generates many calculations. TOC does not trace any costs; it only needs the throughput per unit of product, the time each product uses of the CCR and the company's operating expenses. In cost accounting, we have to add up all the minutes that a product uses of all the resources and in throughput accounting, we only need to know the time each product uses of the CCR.

But the quantity of data is not the most important factor. What is really important is the quality of the information. The information provided by the two approaches is significantly different. We have to conclude which one is better.

First, for the same mix, the profit calculated will be the same for both methodologies, as long as there is no variation in the WIP and the finished good inventories. This is because ABC allocates costs to products and TOC does not. This allocation of costs to products in effect 'stocks' part of the company's expenses in the products, and by doing this it delays their recognition. These stocked expenses will only be recognized when these products are sold. This explains why if the company significantly increases its WIP and/or finished goods during a certain period, its short-term profitability will improve, as a large part of its expenses will be stocked.[56] Because TOC does not aggregate value to WIP and finished goods this does not happen in throughput accounting.

If there is no variation in the stock level, the profits calculated for any mix will be the same with both methodologies, as there will be no stocking of expenses. However, and this is extremely important, the mix chosen is completely different, as we have seen.

If the profit calculated by both methodologies is the same,[57] and if the mix that generated the maximum profit was identified by TOC, we can then conclude that TOC better identifies the most profitable mix.

When we used ABC to calculate the maximum profit the com-

[56] Here we have one of cost accounting's problems: It rewards the increase in the company's WIP and finished goods, which artificially increases the profit of the current period.

[57] The calculated profit is the same, but the paths indicated are completely different, with each leading to different profits and different attitudes, as we will see farther along.

pany could generate, the constraint was not resource C. Remember the definition of a constraint: "anything that limits a system from achieving higher performance in relation to its goal". In this case the constraint was the policy of using ABC. Actually, this is the most common case of constraint in a company (what Goldratt calls policy constraints)! That is to say, we are the ones who impose constraints on the performance of our companies!

ABC did not identify the maximum profit mix, and therefore it did not fulfill one of management accounting's goals. The information provided (of the products' contribution to the company's profitability) was not correct. Therefore, the only possible conclusion is that ABC has a conceptual error in its formation. Some people might argue that the cost drivers were not very well chosen, and that was the reason why ABC did not provide good information. In fact, it does not really matter what cost driver is used; the important thing to realize is that the concept behind cost accounting is wrong, as we will see in the following chapter.

Before we go on there is another important issue. The calculation of a product's cost involves many decisions. Two of the most important decisions are the choice of activities and the choice of cost drivers. The product's total cost depend on these choices. This leads us to conclude that if different activities and/or cost drivers are chosen the product's cost will be different.

Now, how objective is the choice of activities and cost drivers?[58] Would two cost accountants, independently, identify the same activities and/or cost drivers? In other words would they come up with the same product's cost? If you think that they would not come up with the same activities and/or cost drivers then you agree with me that, even if we needed to know the real cost of the products, such a number does not exist! But, fortunately, we do not need it.

[58] The choice of activities and cost drivers are many times influenced by who has more power in an organization, since the choice of different activities and cost drivers will make a product seem more or less profitable.

6

The Damages Caused by Local Optimizations

A company's expenses do not vary according to any cost driver. This is due to the phenomenon that a system has very few constraints and, consequently, most of the system's resources have capacity available to absorb increases in volume and/or changes in mix.

When does a cost vary? When we need to increase the availability of something of which we do not have enough. The costs of an activity should increase only when that activity does not have any excess capacity left, that is, only when that activity becomes a system's constraint or is about to become one.

It does not seem reasonable to assume that all a company's costs will increase when we increase the production volume and/or when we change the production mix, but that is exactly what cost accounting assumes. This is the same as saying that all the variables in a system are equally important for its performance, that all variables are constraints. This assumption is not in line with the concept of a system.

This has recently been recognized by some ABC advocates. "The expense of supplying this resource is incurred, each period, independent of how much of the resource is used."[59] They also recognize that we should not make decisions based on this, "Making decisions based solely upon resource usage (the ABC system) is problematic because there is no guarantee that the spending to supply resources will be aligned with the new levels of resources demanded in the near future . . . Consequently, before making decisions based on an ABC model, managers should analyze the resource supply implications of such decisions."[60]

Even though they do recognize this, they have not abandoned

[59] KAPLAN and COOPER. *Cost and Effect* . . . p. 120.
[60] *Ibid.*, p. 125.

the basic assumption that governs this phenomenon; that local optima leads to global optimum. They still advocate the use of cost drivers to ensure that activities are being efficiently managed. They still try to improve local efficiencies. "The ABC map of product economics highlights the inefficient processes and provides the financial justification for investing in improved processes and fixtures."[61] We have seen an example in chapter 6 where we increase a process's efficiency and, by doing so, we decrease the company's profitability. We have to think of the system as a whole; we cannot try to optimize individual activities. "The obligation of any component is to contribute its best to the system, not to maximize its own production, profit, or sales, nor any other competitive measure. Some components may operate at a loss to themselves in order to optimize the whole system, including the components that take a loss."[62]

Another important assumption of cost accounting is that we can measure the impact of a local decision on the company's bottom line looking primarily at the cost incurred by the decision.

> The cost concept is based on the assumption that 'we can measure the impact of a local area (or local decision) on the bottom line, by measuring how much money this area (or decision) absorbs or releases'. This assumption holds only if we accept that the importance of all things in an organization are in proportion to the operating expense spent on them. Daily life teaches us the opposite. Take for example a case where we run out of a specific material. The damage to the system might be out of proportion to the cost of this material. Or compare the influence on the bottom line of a breakdown of a bottleneck machine to a similar breakdown at a non-constraint machine. The impact is without any relation to the salaries of the workers running them. The mere fact that we intuitively accept the existence of constraints and non-constraints in an organization indicates that we acknowledge the invalidity of the basic assumption of the cost concept.[63]

[61] *Ibid.*, p. 176.

[62] DEMING, W. Edwards. *The New Economics*, Cambridge: Massachusetts Institute of Technology - Center for Advanced Engineering Study 1997. p.97

[63] GOLDRATT, Eliyahu. *The Theory of Constraints Journal*, volume 1, number 2. Avraham Y. Goldratt Institute. 1988, p. 19.

Cost accounting traces the products' consumption of all the activities because of this assumption; as if all the activities had the same importance to the company. "In an activity-based system, the cost of a product is the sum of the costs of all activities required to manufacture and deliver the product."[64]

If we accept that a company is a system, and that every system's performance is limited by very few constraints, then ignoring these constraints will lead to an inability to adequately manage and continuously improve a company. "There really is no choice in this matter. Either you manage constraints or they manage you. The constraints will determine the output of the system whether they are acknowledged and managed or not."[65]

Allocation was initially created to facilitate decision making, to make this process more agile and to improve the quality of the information. When it was created nearly all a firm's costs varied according to the production volume, therefore it supplied relevant information. It still was not correct, but its approximation was good enough. However, the composition of a company's costs has changed significantly, and now most of the costs do not vary according to production volume and/or changes in mix. These costs also do not vary according to any other cost driver. Therefore, allocation is no longer useful. The reason why traditional cost accounting has become obsolete is not the fact that it only uses direct labor as a base for allocation, but because it allocates costs to products.

Today, the people responsible for management accounting (professors, consultants, accountants) do whatever they can, create complicated procedures (that demand tons of data, that take a long time to be implemented, that very few people understand), just to keep allocating costs to products. And even by doing all this they cannot supply relevant information for managers to make decisions. We tend to forget the objective of management accounting, and act as if the objective were to calculate the cost of products!

The mistake of cost accounting is to assume that high local efficiencies lead to global efficiency, that is, if we maximize the individual performance of all the links in the system we will be maximizing the system's global performance. We use allocation and we need cost drivers because of that assumption. The cost drivers are local efficiency measures; they are used to verify that all activities have a good

64 COOPER, R. *The Rise* . . . p. 46,

65 NOREEN and SMITH and MACKEY. *The Theory* . . . p. xix.

local efficiency, to make sure that the company is using all its resources to the maximum. We think that if every resource has a high local efficiency then the system will have a good performance.

The assumption that if we maximize the efficiency of all the system's variables we will be maximizing the system's performance is very ingrained in our thinking. This assumption comes from Scientific Management and, because of that, it is the basis of our management principles. Because we have been using them for quite a while, and because even a great deal of what we learn in universities is based on them, they are not easy to leave aside. To encourage you even more to try and get away from this paradigm, let us see some of the consequences that it has on a company's performance.

6.1. Consequences of Local Optimization on the System's Performance

Maximization of Local Efficiencies—In a plant this appears in the efficiency measurements of the resources; because everyone tries to maximize the efficiency of all the resources, there cannot be any idleness anywhere. When the efficiencies are low there can be some 'interference', after all we are not adequately using our investments. But let us see the results of this quest for high efficiencies.

A plant always has some resources with less capacity than others. Thus, the search for high local efficiencies will cause an increase in WIP without increasing the production volume. Let us use the plant shown below to better visualize this phenomenon.

Figure 6-1
Simple Plant

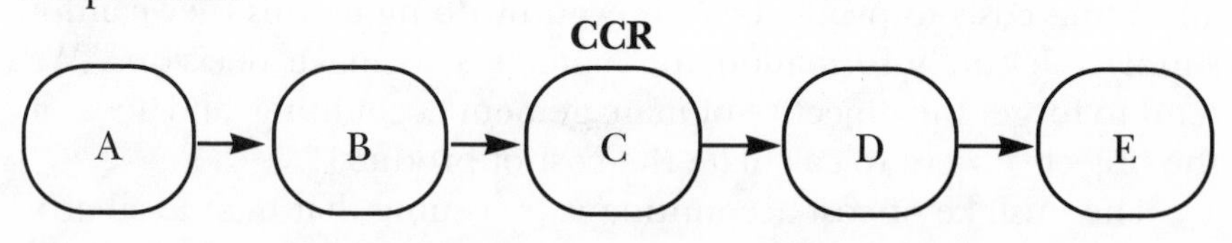

Resource C is this plant's CCR. Let us recall what a CCR is (chapter 3): " In a plant there will always be a resource that limits its maximum flow, as in a chain there always is a weakest link. . . . In a plant the resources that establish the maximum flow are called Capacity Constraint Resource (CCR)". Therefore, resource C is the resource that dictates the maximum flow of this plant.

If this plant has measurements that stimulate local optimizations, the workers will try to use all the resources, all the time. To use resource A all the time it is necessary to feed it until the limit of its capacity. However, resource A has more capacity than resource C, and therefore this will cause the WIP to increase. This in turn increases the company's investment (jeopardizing its cash flow), increases the company's OE, increases the production lead-time (which worsens the customer service) and it does not increase sales (because it is resource C that dictates the flow). Then, we can say that the resources' measurements of local efficiency are something that take the company in the opposite direction of its goal, that is, they decrease the bottom line.

The increase in WIP also causes a decrease in the quality of products and an increase in the delivery performance (as the production lead-times increase). The high WIP will make many resources seem overloaded, and this, along with the constant delays in the promised delivery dates, will result in pressure from clients and will cause unnecessary investments in the plant.[66]

If we try to get 100% efficiency in the nonconstraint resources we will not be increasing throughput (which is limited by the constraint) and we will be increasing WIP. The increase in WIP increases the company's costs. With this we can conclude that it is in the company's interest to have the majority of its resources (which are nonconstraints) idle part of the time. This goes against cost accounting's measurements and it goes against our training.

To make things even worse, many companies impose high local efficiency objectives coupled with measurements that stimulate inventory reductions. Yet, to increase local efficiencies we need to release more raw material to keep the nonconstraint resources working, and by doing this we increase WIP. This shows that it is impossible to have high local efficiencies together with low inventories! This means that many companies (and this likely includes your company) use performance measurements that are conflicting, that do not make sense!

In the above example I used resource efficiency to illustrate some consequences of local optimizations. However, what we are seeing here is also true for any local efficiency measurement.

[66] To better understand how the search for local efficiencies cause these effects (increase in the lead-time, lack of good quality, increase in investments, etc.) read *The Race.*

Therefore it is also true for cost drivers, which are local efficiency measurements of the activities.

Economic Batch [67]—the search for local efficiencies also makes us want to reduce the cost per part. For this we need to find an ideal batch size.

On one side we have the setup costs. If we make a setup that takes many hours and then process only one part, this part will have to absorb all the setup's cost. Therefore, we want to make the maximum number of parts in one setup, which means we want to increase the batch size.

However, the batch size also affects another cost. The bigger the batch size the longer it will stay inside the company, which means that the company will have more carrying costs. Therefore we want to decrease the batch size.

This means that we need to find a batch size that results in the minimum total cost per part, and to do that we use the economic batch size calculation (see graph below).

Figure 6-2

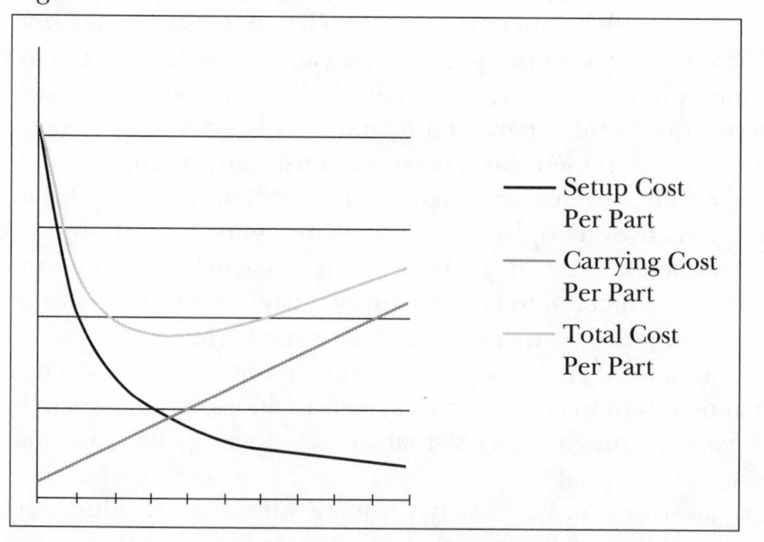

On this graph we have three curves: the setup cost per part, which is the setup cost divided by the number of parts produced in this setup; the carrying cost per part, which is the cost of carrying

[67] For more details on this subject see chapter 4 of *"What is This Thing Called the Theory Of Constraints and How Should It be Implemented?"*

the inventory—a linear increase; and the total cost per part, which is the total of both curves. The economic batch size is the one where the total cost per part is the lowest, in which the total cost per part curve reaches its minimum; this region indicates which batch size minimizes the costs per part.

What we want to do with all of this is reduce the cost per part. To reduce the cost per part we have to, on one side, reduce the setup cost per part, and on the other side, reduce the carrying costs per part. The economic batch size is the technique we use to find a compromise between these two costs. What we are doing is finding out how much we can sacrifice on each one, so that we can reach the minimum cost per unit.

The first thing we should do is verify if we really want to reduce the cost per part. To do that we have to compare the company's goal with this secondary goal. The company's goal is to make money now and in the future. The question here is: If we reduce the cost per part will we be increasing the company's profitability? I will answer this question shortly. For the moment let us assume that the objective of reducing the cost per part is a valid one.

Since we have accepted this secondary objective as valid, we can now analyze the next two steps in our reasoning. We concluded that to reduce the cost per part it is necessary to reduce the setup cost per part. This reasoning implies accepting the setup cost as something normal. Just-In-Time (JIT) showed us that significant reductions in setup are possible in a short time. By doing this, JIT broke our economic batch size reasoning.

However, this is not the only solution. Let's go back to our reasoning. To reduce the cost per part we have to reduce the setup cost per part. Implicit in our reasoning is that a setup costs the company money. Does an extra setup in any company's resource increase the company's OE? Will this make the company spend more money?

According to the setup cost per part curve, the bigger the batch the lower the setup cost per part. Is this right? Where will the batch size affect the company's bottom line? Does a lower setup cost per part really bring any benefit?

What company expense will vary with the size of the production batches? The assumption here is that the smaller the batches, the more setups will be done and, therefore, the greater the company's costs. But this assumption is not valid. To substantiate this statement, let us use the same plant we have just seen as an example.

In this plant, resource C is the CCR. Smaller production batches will cause more setups, but this will not lead to an increase in the company's expenses. Let us assume that currently the batch size policy makes the average setups for resource A to be 3 a week. If we changed this policy to make the average 7 setups a week, the company's expenses would not vary, because resource A is a nonconstraint resource.[68] We do not need to hire another person or buy another resource to perform these extra setups.

The only place where the number of setups affect the company's bottom line is at the constraint. An increase in the number of setups at the constraint would not cause an increase in the company's expenses, but it would cause a decrease in sales, because there would be fewer minutes available for production (this is commonly called *opportunity cost*).

As we have seen, setups do not affect the company's expenses; the only place they have a significant effect is on the CCR. On the nonconstraint resources the batch size does not matter, because we can do hours of setup to produce only one part and this would not have a negative impact on the company's bottom line![69] Therefore, we do not need to calculate and use economic batch sizes. The only place where we want big batches is on the constraint; with the other resources it is better to have smaller batches because in this way the WIP will be smaller (less inventory, lower carrying costs and fewer negative impacts on throughput)[70] and, therefore, lead-time will be shorter (better customer service). This means that curve 1 on the graph preceding creates an illusion! The 'cost world' tries to minimize cost per part by thinking this will contribute to an increase in the company's profitability. But what really matters is not costs per part but the company's costs, and as we have seen, there is no relationship between them.[71]

Cost per Part—The economic batch subject raised another question. Is the objective of reducing costs per part really valid? Let us see an example that illustrates this question.

We are going to analyze proposals from two process engineers.

[68] And with 7 setups a week, resource A is still a nonconstraint resource.

[69] It is obvious that we should not increase the number of setups on the nonconstraint resources to the point where they become a constraint.

[70] For more details see: *The Race* and *Synchronous Manufacturing*, p. 112.

[71] When we minimize the costs per part we are not minimizing the company's costs, sometimes we are actually increasing the company's costs. Costs per part, and therefore product costs, are just a transfer of money inside the system, which does not give any useful information. It just helps to confuse us.

The company's CCR is overloaded and the market would buy more of its products if it could produce more. The company has three resources (A, B and C); they all have one operator, and their costs are the same.

The company sells two products, Blue and Red, whose data are shown below.

Table 6-1

	Blue	**Red**
Price	85	92
Raw Material	37	56
Throughput/Unit	48	36

The current production/sales mix is 50 Blues and 70 Reds a week, and this uses 100% of the available capacity.

The first engineer suggests an improvement in resource A's performance, from 15 minutes/part to 12 minutes/part on product Red. This improvement requires a US$ 5,000 investment.

The second engineer suggests an improvement in resource C's performance, from 21 minutes/part to 20 minutes/part, but with an extra load on resource B, which increase from 6 minutes/part to 9 minutes/part, for the same product Red. This requires an investment of US$ 5,000.

With the objective of reducing the cost per part, what would be the outcome of these two suggestions?

The first engineer suggests reducing the process time of a product on a certain resource in 3 minutes. According to cost accounting "the cost of a product is the sum of the costs of all activities required to manufacture and deliver the product",[72] so this product's cost will decrease, and this suggestion has a great chance of being accepted.

The second engineer suggests reducing the process time of a product by 1 minute on a certain resource, but at the same time increasing this product's process time by 3 minutes on another resource. This means that this engineer is suggesting a 2 minute increase in the process time of a product. Consequently, the product's cost will increase, and the company's OE will increase, due to

[72] COOPER, R. *The Rise . . .* p. 46.

the depreciation of the investment. According to cost accounting this suggestion should be rejected. Most probably this type of suggestion would never be presented in a company with a 'cost world' mentality.

What is wrong with this analysis? First, it does not differentiate between constraint and nonconstraint resources. Without identifying the system's constraint we cannot know if a decision is good or bad. In the preceding case, resource C is the system's constraint, and with this in mind, let us analyze both suggestions.

The first engineer suggests a reduction in the process time of product Red on resource A, a nonconstraint resource, from 15 to 12 minutes/part. This decision will not increase the company's throughput, because resource C limits this plant's output. Now, the company's OE will increase, due to the depreciation of the investment, and the investment will also increase. If throughput is not increasing, and OE and investment are increasing, then the company's profitability will decrease. That is why this suggestion should not be accepted.

The second engineer suggests a reduction in the process time of product Red on the constraint (resource C) in 1 minute. This in turn would increase this product's process time by 3 minutes, on a nonconstraint resource. This decision will increase the company's throughput, as it will free some time from the constraint, which then will be able to increase its production. The decrease of Red's time on the constraint will free 70 minutes on resource C.[73] If these 70 minutes are used to process more Reds, this would increase the production of this product by 3.5 units a week, which would generate an extra US$ 6,552 of throughput a year.[74] The OE will increase by US$ 500 a year, due to the depreciation of the investment, and the investment will increase by US$ 5,000. Now that we have quantified the impact of this suggestion on the three measurements, we can verify if it will increase this company's profitability.

If throughput increases US$ 6,552 and OE increases US$ 500, then the NP will increase US$ 6,052 a year. The investment increases US$ 5,000 therefore, the ROI of this investment is 121% a

[73] With this suggestion, Red will use one minute less on resource C. As this company produces 70 Reds a week, resource C will have an extra 70 minutes available a week, which would enable the company to increase its production volume.

[74] Increase in the weekly throughput = 3.5 x 36 = US$ 126. Increase in the annual throughput = US$ 126 x 52 weeks = US$ 6,552.

year. This suggestion would certainly be accepted by throughput accounting.

We increased the cost per part of a product and we significantly improved the company's performance. This shows that the objective of minimizing cost per part is not a valid one if you want to optimize the whole system. The cost per part is just another illusion created by the search for local optimizations, what Goldratt calls a "mathematical phantom". This explains why the cost of setup per part curve in the economic batch graph creates an illusion.

When we minimize the costs per part we are not minimizing the company's costs. Sometimes we are actually increasing its costs, and minimization does not inform us about the impact on the firm's throughput. The cost per part, and therefore product cost, is just an internal transfer of money that does not provide any information about the impact of a decision on the company's bottom line. In fact, it has a negative impact, because it creates wrong perceptions in our minds, which leads us to make wrong decisions.

The case we have just examined is an example of this. The search for lower cost per part resulted in approval of a suggestion that worsened the company's profitability, and rejection of a suggestion that significantly improved the company's performance. This, on its own, is significant, but there is another important factor.

The first engineer was rewarded and thinks he contributed to the company's goal. While the second engineer was most likely fired! However, it is very improbable that in a company with cost accounting mentality, someone would have come up with a suggestion like the second one, which is one of the devastating effects of this mentality. We end up thinking we contributed to the company's goal, and we are rewarded for that, when we really worsened the situation. Meanwhile suggestions that really improve the company's performance never emerge, because we are not stimulated to think about the company as a whole.

In chapter 5 we saw the example of company RS, where the costs per part led us to make the wrong decisions, decisions that are not in line with the company's goal. Going back to this example, in tables 9 and 16, shown as follows, we can see that when allocating the costs of resources A and D, product R was the product that received the majority of the costs. This is because product R is the one that uses these resources the most. Nevertheless, the other table shows that these resources have idle time—they are nonconstraints. This means that if we want to increase product's R volume, we do not really need to increase the expenses associated with resources A and D, but even so, cost accounting still informs us that these costs will vary if we increase production of product R. Before the costs with resources A and D vary, we have to elevate the constraint, resource C. But cost accounting does not identify the constraint, so it cannot know when the costs will vary. This is an extremely important conclusion. In turn it leads us to the conclusion that if we want to control our costs we have to control the system's constraints (we will go back to this point later on).

Table 6-2

Resource	Minutes necessary for R	Minutes necessary for S	Total necessary minutes	Necessary minutes/available minutes
A	780	390	1,170	48.8%
B	910	455	1,365	56.9%
C	**1,040**	**1,820**	**2,860**	**119.2%**
D	910	455	1,365	56.9%

Table 6-3
Use of the Resources by the Products (Minutes)

	R	S
A	6	3
B	7	3.5
C	8	14
D	7	3.5
Total	**28**	**24**

The constraint in this case is the time of resource C. What is the relevance of product R using more of the time of resources A and D, if they are nonconstraints? The costs of these resources will not vary while the constraint is another resource. The utilization of resource C is the key factor here, and in this case, product R is the product that least uses this resource! And cost accounting does not take this into account either. Cost accounting simply ignores the existence of the system's constraint.

In this same example, if we decided to stop producing product R (which, after all, according to cost accounting was losing money), we would not cut most of the expenses allocated to this product. The only cost that would certainly not be incurred any longer would be the raw material costs. In this case, if we stopped producing this product, the company's profitability would decrease, as we saw in chapter 5. It is as if cost accounting is saying that product R is a product that loses money, but if we stop producing it the company's bottom line would worsen—this does not make any sense! If the costs allocated to product R are still incurred even if we stop producing it, how can we say these costs are product R's costs?

This leads us to another undesirable effect of the allocation of costs to products. This allocation creates the false impression that we will not incur the allocated costs if we stop producing the products. This is not true, because we will not stop having part of a machine if we stop producing one of the many products that are processed on it.[75]

What ABC advocates might say is that by increasing the efficiency of an activity you are creating future opportunities to:

- Reduce cost by eliminating the excess capacity created by the increase in efficiency.
- Increase throughput by using this excess capacity to sell more products/services.

The point is that you might be creating these opportunities, but it does not assure you that these will be an improvement on the system's performance. Apart from that, sometimes, as we have already seen, by increasing local efficiencies you might be decreasing profitability. Therefore, you should only make local improvements if you know you will improve the global performance. If this were not true, anything could be locally improved because of potential long-term global improvements and this would also disperse the managers' efforts, since you can improve local efficiencies everywhere.

Corporations—Before we continue, we have to see the consequences of the search for local efficiencies on the evaluation of companies that are part of a corporation. In chapter 4 we saw how TOC evaluates plants from a corporation. Here we will see how cost accounting does that, and what it entails.

[75] To see how TOC deals with the pruning of products, see the example in chapter 4 in this book.

Cost accounting allocates the headquarters OE between the various plants to measure their performance. Most of the time I came across this problem the variable used to allocate this OE was the plant's (division's) revenues. They would calculate each plant's percentage in the overall revenues, and then would allocate the headquarters OE using this proportion. The assumption here is that if a plant increases its revenues then it will cause an increase in the headquarters OE, or vice-versa. This relationship does not exist. Imagine this: if the revenues of one plant decreased and the revenues of all the other plants stayed the same, would the headquarters OE decrease? Of course not!

This methodology simply involves internal transfer of money, which will have no impact on the system's overall performance. In this system, when a plant's revenues decrease and the revenues of the other plants stay the same, the amount of OE that goes to this company falls. What happens is that the amount of OE taken from this one plant is distributed (allocated) to the other plants, which will cause a decrease in the NP of the other plants; yet all this internal money transfer did not change the overall profit one cent. The companies that did not change their revenues saw an increase in their part of the headquarters OE, and will receive poor evaluations.

Any allocation will lead us to mistakes no matter what variable is chosen, or even if many variables are chosen. Any allocation creates local optimizations and these are not good for the system as a whole.

I have seen situations where a company has increased its sales without significantly increasing its own OE, but its NP, calculated by headquarters (after the allocation of the headquarters OE) had decreased! The company received a bad evaluation because the corporation's management thought that that specific plant was not contributing to the corporation's NP. This happened because the other companies had decreased their sales, and this caused an increase in the company's share of the headquarters OE (which remained the same). Why is this so illogical? Because the company increased its sales without increasing its own OE, and all the extra throughput that came in from this increase in sales went directly to the NP; it was all fresh money that the company brought into the system. If you had removed the headquarters OE from the analysis, the company's NP would have more than tripled, that is, the company was bringing a lot of fresh money into the system, but the system thought that that company was losing money.

Let us use the example from chapter 4, of the three plants, to better illustrate this situation.

The amounts of the headquarters' OE allocated to each unit, as a factor of each unit's sales, is as follows.

Table 6-4
Allocation of Headquarters OE—August

	Sales	%	Headquarters OE
CompuCar	570,080	11.2%	18,654
ElectroHome	1,786,203	35.2%	58,449
GoodSound	2,711,120	53.5%	88,714
	5,067,403	100%	165,817

With this, the NP of the plants and the corporations are:

Table 6-5
Corporate Results—August

Unit	Throughput	% Total	Oper. Exp.	NP	% Total	Invest.	%	ROI
CompuCar	310,840	12.5%	265,608	45,232	48.3%	5,000,000	28.9%	10.9%
ElectroHome	843,518	34%	783,490	60,028	64%	8,000,000	46.2%	9.0%
GoodSound	1,323,420	53.4%	1,334,938	–11,518	–12.3%	4,300,000	24.9%	-3.2%
Total	2,477,778	100%	2,384,036	**93,742**	100%	17,300,000	100%	

Invest in headquarters	250,000
Total Investment	17,550,000
Total ROI	**6.4%**

According to this analysis, GoodSound is losing money. This conclusion is the opposite of the one we reached when using TOC to do the analysis, where GoodSound was the company that most contributed to the corporation's NP. It went from profit to loss because it was the company that received the largest part of the headquarters OE, given that it has the highest sales of the three plants.

Therefore, if GoodSound continues in this state, we should close it or sell it to stop the system from hemorrhaging. But, the notion that this company is losing money is wrong. The part of the headquarters OE allocated to GoodSound does not make much sense. If the company was no longer part of the corporation, would the 53.5% of the headquarters OE be eliminated? Of course not! Then, how can we say that this is an OE of this company? If this company were no longer part of the corporation, the overall performance of the system would be highly jeopardized.

The end result reached by TOC and by cost accounting is the same. But, the analysis of the plants' performances is very different. The difference is that cost accounting does internal money transfers (allocation), and this causes very serious distortions in the performance measurements.

6.2 Conclusion

As we have seen, the search for local optima leads to negative consequences for the company. The local performance measurements are in conflict with the global goal.

A significant difference between TOC and the costing methodologies is what each methodology defines as productivity. For TOC something is productive only when it helps the system to move towards its goal, and because the goal of an industry is to make money now and in the future, an increase in productivity occurs only when the company's profitability increases. The "cost world" searches for local efficiencies, which results in statements like: "In a certain area we increased productivity by X%." You cannot have an increase in productivity in only one area; if there is an increase in productivity in one area it is an increase for the whole system.[76] TOC is concerned with the system as a whole, it is concerned with aligning local decisions with the global goal. Here's how one author advocates reform.

> We need a new mathematics for productivity. The goal of this new mathematics for productivity is to improve the perform-

[76] See chapter 4 of *The Goal.*

[77] LORINO, P. O. *Economista e o Administrador, Elementos de Microeconomia para uma Nova Gestão.* São Paulo: Livraria Nobel, 1992, p. 75, my translation.

> mance of the set of resources as a whole. It is based on organizational techniques adapted to this objective, which constitute, progressively, a new body of knowledge for companies, and which are the key for modern competitiveness, as Taylor's scientific management was before.[77]

Another consequence of trying to minimize costs per part is that it stimulates an increase in WIP and finished goods inventories, because in doing so, managers can artificially increase the company's profits in the short-run. When you allocate costs to products, what you are doing is delaying the recognition of these allocated expenses. Thus, the profit of one period increases while the profits of future periods are jeopardized.

The search for local optima causes a dispersion of efforts in the opposite direction of the company's goal. These goals only disperse effort:

- Maximizing local efficiencies
- Having economic batch sizes
- Minimizing costs per part

In fact they are some of the illusions resulting from the search for local optima. These goals give us the impression that if we achieve them we will achieve a good global performance, but as we saw, this is not true. We can therefore conclude that local optima do not lead to global optimum.

The salient difference between throughput accounting and the cost accounting methodologies is found in this basic assumption. Cost accounting methodologies consider this assumption valid, that is, if we want a good overall performance for the system all we need to do is optimize the various links of the system. On the other hand one of the basic assumptions of TOC is quite the opposite: that local optima do not lead to global optimum. Thus, a system that tries to optimize all its links is a very inefficient system. These two different perceptions constitute what Goldratt calls the "Cost World" and the "Throughput World."

The "cost world" does not recognize the interdependencies between the links. This gives us the false impression that to manage well, all you have to do is optimize all company activities. That is why ABC (and the other cost methodologies) need so much data, because everything is equally important. In the examples of how to use throughput accounting statements, we saw that managing according to the throughput world demands much less data and is much easier.

If your goal is to manage the system it is much easier if you admit that dependencies exist, that linkages between the various variables of the system exist. When we admit that these interdependencies exist, we perceive that the company's performance is dictated by very few variables (constraints), and that, consequently, we can manage it adequately, controlling these few variables. The cost world is our attempt to break these linkages, to make management easier.

Still, local optima are not bad by nature. Let us analyze this point. Optimization only has any meaning when related to an objective that we want to maximize. Then, local optima only make sense if we also have local objectives. In the same way, global optimum only make sense if we have a global objective. So, we want to maximize local areas according to these areas' local objectives, and we want to maximize the system as a whole according to this system's objective.

That said, we can go back to the assumption: Local optima do not lead to global optimum. Behind this assumption is another assumption, which states that: The local areas' objectives are in conflict with the system's objective. Only then will local optimizations not contribute to the system's performance.

For example: In most plants there is a local objective of producing the maximum possible on each resource. This is why there are local efficiency measurements. This local objective, as we saw, is in conflict with the global objective. But if we change the local objective to: "The objective of a local area is to contribute positively to the objective of the global organization"[78] then there would be no problem in searching for local optima, because they would then be subordinated to the global optimum. The important thing is that each area's goal is subordinated to the system's goal.

[78] GOLDRATT, E. *The Theory* . . . p. 7.

7

Criticisms of Throughput Accounting

7.1. Short-Term v. Long-Term

The biggest criticism of TOC's accounting is that it is oriented towards the short-term.

> TOC . . . is persuasive and logically correct given the problem it set out to solve. This problem is how to maximize throughput when the organization has a fixed supply of resources, when its expenses and spending for the next period—other than materials—have already been determined, when its products have already been designed, when its prices have been set, and when its customers orders have been received.[79] We do not say that the assumptions underlying TOC are invalid. They are an excellent approximation of reality for the problem TOC has been designed to solve: short-term product mix and scheduling of bottleneck resources.[80]

As we have seen in the many examples in this book, this is a mistaken view of TOC.

The cost world promoters say that in the short-run expenses do not vary with the production volume or with any other cost driver, but that in the long-run they do.

> We need to eliminate the mentality that fixed costs are necessary for production, but are not influenced by our product and production decisions. Once we accept that virtually all product costs are variable over some reasonable time period,

[79] KAPLAN and COOPER. *Cost and Effect* . . . p. 132.
[80] *Ibid.*, p. 134.

> then it becomes necessary to do whatever we can to understand the sources of all overhead costs and to trace them to the activities that drive these costs. We must abandon conventional rules that either ignore fixed costs (the direct cost approach) or allocate them on an arbitrary, usually dysfunctional, basis (the full cost approach).[81]

As Johnson and Kaplan stated, the ABC defenders say all costs are variable in the long-run, and because of that we have to identify the long-run costs of the products to be able to make good decisions. It is true that costs vary in the long-run, and we should not ignore this fact as direct costing does. In past years what many called fixed costs were actually the costs that were growing. But we would be wrong to believe that we need to calculate the long-term cost of products to be able to make good decisions. As we have seen in the many examples in this book, TOC does not calculate any product cost and yet was able to make better decisions than ABC. There is no management decision that we cannot make without the cost of products. We can make any decision without this so-called "mathematical phantom". In fact we should never use it, because not only does it not provide good information, it also leads managers to make decisions that jeopardize the company's performance.

In the long-run the company will continue to be a system and, therefore, it will still have its performance limited by very few constraints. Therefore, even in the long-run, it is necessary to identify and control the constraints, and not ignore them thinking that in the long-run all resources are equally important. When the 'cost world' states that it is necessary to calculate the long-run costs of the products, it is stating that, in the long-run, all the company's resources will be constraints at the same time and because of that, all resources are equally important, as if in the long-run local optima were good for the system.

What has not been understood is that TOC can be used in long-term decisions. All we have to do is use the five focusing steps to determine the system's future constraints. If we increase a decision's time horizon we are able to view its impact in the company's future. As a matter of fact this must be done in order to know and control a company's future available capacity. But if we use a management system that does not identify the system's constraints, exploit them,

[81] JOHNSON and KAPLAN. *Relevance Lost* . . . p. 243.

subordinate all other resources/activities to the constraints, elevate the constraints and then find the new constraints, how can we improve in the short or the long-run? Remember, whenever we use TOC's five focusing steps, we are improving the system's performance. Since we are supposed to use this process continuously, we will be improving the system's performance in the short and the long-term.

> In TOC, the default assumption is that overhead functions, like other nonconstraint work centers, can handle additional diversity without new resources. If they cannot, the overhead resources themselves become the constraint and can be dealt with using the usual TOC approaches. That is, improvement efforts can be focused on that part of overhead that is the constraint . . . At the sites we visited very few managers seemed concerned about problems of creeping overhead. For the most part, they seemed to be able to diversify and increase volume with relatively modest increases in overhead."[82]

Noreen, Smith and Mackey's research on TOC shows that the companies that use TOC are able to increase their diversity of products and their production volume without increasing overhead. This goes against the cost world literature, as Noreen, Smith and Mackey have observed:

> Managers at almost all of the sites we visited claimed that they had been able to reduce or keep operating expenses constant despite increased volumes and variety. This fact is surprising given the assertions made in the ABC literature concerning the effects of volume and variety on overhead costs.[83]

The overhead expenses will only vary when at least one of their components becomes a constraint. If a company has good control over its constraints, and optimize their use, it will be able to increase

82 NOREEN, E., SMITH, D. and MACKEY, J. *The Theory of Constraints* and its *Implications for Management Accounting*. Great Barrington: North River Press, 1995, p. xxvii.

83 *Ibid.*, p. 144.

its performance without increasing overhead. The current problem is that companies do not identify and explore their constraints and this leads to unnecessary increases in overhead. One of the main reasons for the long-run variations of the overhead costs is the fact that managers do not have the company's constraints under control. In other words, the fact that managers use cost accounting is what causes the company's costs to increase!

This fact does not show up much in the TOC literature, but it is extremely important, especially because many criticisms of TOC argue that the theory does not control costs and that it has a short-term perspective. Let us explore this point a bit more. I stated that the use of cost accounting leads to higher costs. How can I say that? We saw that the search for local optima increases WIP, increases investment in machines, leads to poor quality and bad customer service. It also makes us reject good improvement suggestions while accepting bad suggestions, and provides erroneous information about the products' profitability. All these factors increase the company's costs.[84]

"In the 'throughput world,' constraints are the essential classification, replacing the role that products played in the 'cost world.'"[85] By controlling the company's constraints, we can avoid the growth of the so-called fixed costs.

One of the main mistakes people make when analyzing TOC is to think that it maintains expenses do not vary. "In this view, operating expenses are unrelated to decisions made about product sold and customers served."[86] TOC does not assume that overhead costs are necessary for production and that they are not affected by our decisions. First of all, TOC does not classify costs as variable or fixed, but as totally variable and not totally variable. It seems a minor difference, but this classification does not force us to try and find a way of forecasting how the costs are going to behave. According to TOC the time to analyze the cost variation is when we have to make a decision. Each decision has to be analyzed by taking into consideration its impact on the three measurements: throughput, investment and operating expense. TOC's assumption is that we can verify the impact of the decisions on the company's expenses on a case-by-case

[84] To have a better understanding on how the cost world mentality increases the costs of a company, read: *The Race* and *Synchronous Manufacturing* p. 40.

[85] GOLDRATT, E. *The Haystack* . . . p. 57.

[86] KAPLAN and COOPER. *Cost and Effect* . . . p. 132.

basis. This assumption eliminates the need to find activities and cost drivers to try and measure the variability of costs in relation to the products. What we have to do is analyze the variation of costs in relation to a decision.

What makes a cost vary is a decision made by the company's managers. In whatever period being analyzed, short or long-term, the company will always have at least one constraint (if this were not true its profit would be infinite). It is obvious that the constraint can change places, move from one machine to another, or shift to the market, or whatever. However, if we do not identify where it is, we will not be able to significantly improve the company's performance and will not even be able to control the costs, be it in the short or the long-run.

As we have seen, if a company uses cost accounting it will make decisions that decrease its profitability, which might make the company's future unfeasible!

But the most important point is that cost accounting and throughput accounting have two very different and conflicting management philosophies. These two different management philosophies will lead the company to very different paths, and here is where the short-run versus long-run argument should focus. The point is, which of the two management philosophies will lead to a more competitive long-term position? I will answer this question in chapter 10.

7.2. Throughput Accounting and Other Methodologies

At a first glance, Throughput Accounting (TA) seems to be very similar to other methodologies, even like direct costing and linear programming. These two methodologies are mentioned in cost accounting books, the first one being considered very short-sighted and the second one not mentioned very much, but also considered of very short-term use.

This impression may be due to the fact that TA does not allocate indirect costs, which direct costing also does not do, and because TA also calculates the throughput per time of the CCR, which linear programming does do. However, the similarities between these two methodologies and TA end here.

One of the main arguments against direct costing is that it neglects fixed costs. TA does not do that, because in order to verify whether a decision being made will increase a company's profitability it quantifies the decision's impact on the company's OE.

Moreover, we already saw that if the company is managed according to TOC principles, it will have better control over its costs.

The measurement used by TA to identify the products that most contribute to the company's profits (when the constraint is the plant's CCR), the throughput per time of CCR, is the same measurement advocated by linear programming. However, linear programming does not offer other measurements nor does it offer a substitute for cost accounting; it is simply a tool to be used in many circumstances. One of the main arguments against linear programming is that it is useful only in the very short-term, given that constraints do not last long. As we have already seen, there will always be at least one constraint, because if this were not true the company's profit would be infinite. The constraint is not always a machine; many times it is the market, when the company cannot sell everything it is able to produce. TOC has approaches that deal with physical or policy constraints.

Apart from that, even though these aspects have been taken into account before, TOC has shown that they are much more important than we thought. Still, the main difference between TA and these and other methodologies is the paradigm shift from the 'cost world' to the 'throughput world'. The other methodologies are still based on the prevailing paradigm; they do not force us to change our perceptions in relation to the management of a business (we will discuss these points later on).

TA is much more in line with the financial analysis of investments. What really matters is not an internal flow of money but the system's exchange of money with the outside world. Have you noticed how, when we are going to decide to build a plant or increase the capacity of an existing plant, we use cash-flow concepts and incremental analysis, and after the decision is made, we evaluate the investment based on cost accounting?

7.3. Throughput Accounting and Production Logistics

Some people criticize TA because it is very dependent on production logistics. Without a significant change in the way the production is managed a company cannot use TA. This assertion is absolutely correct. But I do not consider this assertion negative.

Whatever the management accounting system, it should be intimately connected with production management. Without this it will not be able to provide good information for decision making. In my view, this is one of the biggest problems with cost accounting. More and more, it is moving away from production management—cost accountants are not supposed to know much about production! How can we measure and evaluate a system if we do not know how it works?

I hope that by now the fundamental role of the company's CCR in its performance is clear. It dictates the plant's maximum flow and the products' contributions to the company's profitability. This means that if, for any reason, the CCR shifts, that is, if another resource becomes the company's CCR, the products' contributions to the company's profitability (their throughput per time of the CCR) might change completely. This has a huge impact on the company's strategies, because the sales mix and the products contribution to profit (throughput/time of CCR) can (and most probably will) completely change if the CCR shifts. A product that previously contributed heavily to the company's profitability (and consequently the company stimulated its sale) may become an unimportant product (with a low throughput/time of CCR), and vice-versa.

To avoid this scenario we must not allow the CCR to move. This leads us to a very important point, which I will only deal with briefly, and this is the strategic choice of the CCR.

There are some points where it is better, strategically, to position the CCR. The cost in increasing the resource's capacity is one factor that should be taken into account. It is more important to position the CCR on a resource where increases in capacity are very expensive—on a resource that has a high investment value. It does not make much sense to limit the whole plant's performance with the capacity of a resource where investments are inexpensive. Apart from the amount of the investment, the CCR's position in the plant's process flow is also important. There are some resources and positions in the process flow that complicate the plant's management, and, therefore, should not be the CCR.

Another point to take into consideration is the potential market for the company's products. It would be wise to have the CCR on a resource where the products that have the most market potential are also the most profitable products.

For a company that is building a plant, these are some key factors that it should take into consideration. For the plants that are already working, the identification of CCRs is imperative.[87] We also

[87] In some cases it is possible to choose the CCR's location, even when the plant is already in production.

have to control production in a way such that the CCR will not shift and whereby we will be able to guarantee that the non-CCR resources have enough protective capacity.[88] Changes in the CCR should be a management decision, not an accident.

Because of these reasons, throughput accounting should only be used when there is a good production management system.[89] I do not believe this is a weak point of TA. To the contrary, it is a strong point, because it will help a management accounting system to provide good and useful information (and for most companies this will happen for the first time).

[88] For a definition of protective capacity see the appendix.

[89] For more details on TOC's production logistics methodology, see: *The Race*, *Synchronous Manufacturing* and *Self-Learning Kit.*

8
Other Decisions Using TOC

In chapter 4 we saw how to use the TA statements to make decisions. In this chapter we will see some examples of how to use TA to make other types of decisions.

8.1. Pricing

To determine prices, many companies still use product costs, adding a profit margin to the calculated cost to determine a 'fair' price. The idea of only one fair price restricts the company's performance a lot (as we will see later on). We should not use the erroneous concept of product cost to stipulate prices. In fact, we should not use the company's internal data about how to make products to determine the prices. We should listen to the market and price products according to the market's perception of value.

If we are not going to use the company's internal data to price products, what is management accounting's role? It should inform managers if the stipulated prices, at a determined sales volume, will increase the company's profitability. In other words, management accounting must inform managers if it is worthwhile to produce and sell the products at these prices and volumes and with the new sales mix.

Using TA statements we have two methods that can easily perform this kind of analysis. The first one needs the following inputs from marketing and sales: estimated price, sales volume and new sales mix. To show how this works out, let us use the example of company Right-Time, when its CCR is overloaded (chapter 4).

The production and sales of a new product, Stars, are being analyzed. The product has a forecasted TVC of US$ 45 and a forecasted time on the CCR of 9 minutes. The necessary investment to get it to market is US$ 15,000 and the OE will increase US$ 500 a month.

The marketing and sales people estimate that at a sales price of US$ 145, the market will buy 120 units a month. Let us see if this would increase the company's profitability.

Table 8-1
Simulation—Data Base of Products

Product	Price	TVC	Throughput per Unit (Tu)	Time on CCR (min)	Tu/Min on CCR
Lady	68	42	26	0	
Classic	120	35	85	5	**17.00**
Goldstar	343	134	209	15	**13.93**
Sportsman	254	71	183	15	**12.20**
Yacht	147	56	91	8	**11.38**
Stars	145	45	100	9	**11.11**
Kids	35	4	31	3	**10.33**
Champion	97	42	55	7	**7.86**

The new product has a Tu/minute on CCR of US$ 11.11. To produce 120 units a month we need 1,080 minutes of the CCR's time. Since the CCR is overloaded we need to reduce the production of other product(s).

Thus far, we can say that if we free time on the CCR by reducing production of a product that has a higher Tu/minute of CCR than product 'Stars' has, we would be reducing the company's profitability. This point is extremely important because it shows that the data on the new product is not the only one needed to make the decision to sell it or not, given that the new mix has the power to change the profitability outcome. The decision of what product to stop producing in order to make the new product is fundamental. Depending on this choice the new product release may or may not increase the company's profitability, if the new product is substituting a product that has a higher Tu/minute of the CCR then it will reduce the company's bottom line.

Below we have the analysis for this example:

Table 8-2
Simulation
Capacity of CCR = 10,032   Demand/CCR capacity = 122.3%

Product	Demand (Forecast)	Maximum Throughput Mix	Sales Mix	Acum. Utiliz. of CCR %		Total Throughput per Product	
Lady	660	660	660	0.0%	0.0%	17,160	17,160
Classic	420	420	420	20.9%	20.9%	35,700	35,700
Goldstar	110	110	110	37.4%	37.4%	22,990	22,990
Sportsman	250	250	225	74.8%	71.0%	45,750	41,175
Yacht	200	200	120	90.7%	80.6%	18,200	10,920
Stars	120	103	70	100%	86.9%	10,300	7,000
Kids	300	0	42	100%	88.1%	0	1,302
Champion	170	0	170	100%	100%	0	9,350

	Total Throughput	150,100	145,597
Variation in OE = 500	Operating Expense	12,835	112,835
	Net Profit	37,265	32,762
	(NP difference)	4,503	
	NP difference between analyzed alternatives		–962
	Investment necessary		15,000
	Proposal's ROI (annual)		–77%
	Investment	2,115,000	2,115,000
	ROI (annual)	21.1%	18.6%

With the new sales mix the company's profitability decreases, and we will not be able to deliver the entire market demand for the new product. The NP went from US$ 33,724 to US$ 32,762, and because the OE and the investment increased, the company's ROI declined by nearly 1%. The problem here is that in order to produce the new product we stopped producing more profitable products, which shows how important the product mix is in the company's decisions. The fact that the new sales mix decreases the company's profitability in the period being analyzed should not be enough to reject the idea. Sometimes, the launching of new products is a marketing necessity. After all, if the company does not innovate it runs the risk of losing more money in the future than it will lose now. To better analyze this issue we can expand the forecast horizon: instead of simulating only a month we can simulate a year or more. This will show us if it is worthwhile to include the new product in the company's offerings at the moment.

If in the case above the company's CCR were not overloaded, the result would be different, as it would not be necessary to decrease the supply of any other product. Therefore, if the extra throughput earned with the new product exceeded the extra OE by an amount sufficient to compensate for the extra investment, the inclusion of the new product in the company's offerings would increase its profitability.

The other method that helps us in pricing products goes from bottom to top. We use the company's NP and ROI to measure its performance in relation to its goal. Therefore we can start this kind of analysis by establishing what ROI we want and from then on, we will get to the price we should charge for the new product. Then the marketing and sales people have to decide if it is possible to sell the product at this price and volume. If they conclude that the market will not pay this price, this means that only a lower price and/or volume would be accepted, and consequently the target ROI would not be met.

Let us suppose that the target ROI is the same as the company's current ROI, so the analysis will show the minimum price the company should charge the product to, at least, maintain its profitability. To illustrate this other method we will use the same example, but now we do not have a price for the new product beforehand.

The company is analyzing the introduction of a new product, Stars, in its offerings. This new product has a (forecasted) TVC of US$ 45. It also has a (forecasted) use of the CCR of 9 minutes. The company will have to invest US$ 15,000 and the OE will increase by US$ 500 a month. The predicted sales volume is 70 units a month and, as the company's CCR is overloaded, the production of the products Sportsman, Yacht and Kids will be reduced by 25, 29 and 8 units, respectively.

The company's current ROI is 19.3%. The investment will therefore increase by US$ 15,000 and in order to maintain the same ROI the company's NP must increase by US$ 241.25 a month, which results in a monthly NP of US$ 33,965.25. As OE will be US$ 112,835 a month, the company's throughput has to be US$ 146,800.25 (US$ 741.25 higher). Since we know how much total throughput the company has to generate, and we know the total throughput generated by all products aside from the new product, we can calculate what the new product's total throughput should be. Then, if we divide this total throughput by the new product's volume, we will find the price for this product that will maintain the company's profitability. Below we have the calculation of product Stars's total throughput.

Table 8-3

Capacity of CCR = 10,032 Demand/CCR capacity = 117.8

Product	Demand (Forecast)	Sales Mix	Acum. Utiliz. of CCR %	Total Throughput per Product
Lady	660	660	0.0%	17,160
Classic	420	420	20.9%	35,700
Goldstar	110	110	37.4%	22,990
Sportsman	250	225	71.0%	41,175
Yacht	200	120	80.6%	10,920
Kids	300	42	81.8%	1,302
Champion	170	170	93.7%	9,350
Stars	70	70	100%	?

Variation in OE = 500

Total Throughput	146,800
Operating Expense	112,835
Net Profit	33,965
NP difference between analyzed alternatives	241
Investment necessary	15,000
Proposal's ROI (annual)	19.3%
Investment	2,115,000
ROI (annual)	19.3%

Stars's total throughput has to be US$ 8,203.25. For the product's 70 units to generate this amount of throughput, the product's unitary throughput has to be US$ 117.19. Since its TVC is US$ 45, its selling price has to be US$ 162.19, which results in a Tu/minute of CCR of US$ 13.02. The Data Base of Products would be:

Table 8-4
Data Base of Products

Product	Price	TVC	Throughput per Unit (Tu)	Time on CCR (min)	Tu/Min on CCR
Lady	68	42	26	0	
Classic	120	35	85	5	17.00
Goldstar	343	134	209	15	13.93
Stars	162.19	45	117.19	9	13.02
Sportsman	254	71	183	15	12.20
Yacht	147	56	91	8	11.38
Kids	35	4	31	3	10.33
Champion	97	42	55	7	7.86

The marketing people can now verify if the market will buy the product at this price. The goal here should be to check if the company can charge more for the product, because then the company's profitability would increase.

Here, again, we see the importance of the sales mix, which is the key factor in this kind of analysis. If we had reduced the supply of the company's current products in another way, product Stars's minimum price would have been another value. Often, it is advisable to create several simulations, using several different sales mixes.

This makes it even more clear that managers have to manage the company's capacity, and to be able to do that they need to manage its CCR. By doing that they will also be controlling the company's costs, and not allowing its OE to increase disproportionately. We can manage a complex system focusing on few links. This explains the errors of the product cost concept, which does not take into account the fact that a system's performance is determined by few links, and also does not take into account the company's available capacity.

We saw two methods to make decisions about pricing, and the first method is the most recommended one. This is because the second method is more susceptible to forecasting errors since we are starting with a scenario in which we do not have the price but have to stipulate the sales volume. Moreover, we are stipulating a minimum price to marketing, which goes against the idea that it is the market that establishes the price. However, when marketing is unable to estimate a price based on the market (for example, when the product is completely innovative, without any similar product in the market), the second method is the only one, of the two, that can help.

8.2. Launching of New Products

Launching a new product can affect the offering of other products when the company's CCR is overloaded. In this case we have to determine which product will see its production reduced in order to then quantify the impact of this launching on the company's bottom line. This type of analysis is very similar to the analysis we have seen, so I will complicate the situation slightly.

The company wants to launch a new product, and has two alternatives: it can launch either product Soft or Smooth. It does not want to launch both products for marketing reasons. We have to decide between these two products (or we can decide not to launch either of them). Let us see how we should make this decision.

Before launching one of the new products the company has two products, Normal and Hard, whose data is shown below:

Table 8-5

Product	**Price**	**TVC**	**Throughput per Unit (Tu)**	**Time on CCR (min)**	**Tu/Min on CCR**
Normal	85	35	50	10	**10.00**
Hard	72	57	15	5	**3.00**

The weekly demand is 120 units for Normal and 300 units for Hard. The CCR is available 2,400 minutes a week, and the OE is US$

9,000 a week. Below we have the calculation of the company's maximum NP.

Because Normal is the one that most contributes to the company's profitability, we are first going to produce and sell everything the market demands of it, and then, if there is time left on the CCR. we will produce and sell product Hard.

Table 8-6
Maximum Profit Mix
CCR Capacity = 2,400 Demand/CCR capacity = 112.5%

Product	Demand (Forecast)	Maximum Throughput Mix	Acum. Utiliz. of CCR %	Total Throughput per Product
Normal	120	120	50%	6,000
Hard	300	240	100%	3,600

Total Throughput	9,600
Operating Expense	9,000
Net Profit	**600**

The demand for Normal is 120 units a week, and as each unit uses 10 minutes of the CCR, we will use 1,200 minutes of our constraint. Thus, we still have another 1,200 minutes available to produce Hard. Given that each Hard uses 5 minutes of the CCR, we can make 240 units. Therefore we have a maximum profit mix of 120 Normal + 240 Hard.

The company's total throughput with this mix is US$ 9,600, which, with an OE US$ 9,000, results in a weekly profit of US$ 600.

Now we want to know if we should launch a new product, and we have two alternatives: product Soft or Smooth. We need to know which one maximizes the company's profitability. Products Soft and Smooth have a throughput per unit of 40 and 70, and use 10 and 20 minutes of the CCR, respectively. Therefore, their Tu/minute of the CCR are US$ 4 and US$ 3.5. The demand for Soft is 10 and of Smooth is 20 units a week. In the table below we have the data for these two products.

Table 8-7
Data Base of Products

Product	Price	TVC	Throughput per Unit (Tu)	Time on CCR (min)	Tu/Min on CCR
Soft	160	120	40	10	**4.00**
Smooth	235	165	70	20	**3.50**

If we consider only the products' Tu/minute of CCR we decide to produce Soft. The company's new Data Base of Products and the maximum profit mix are shown below:

Table 8-8
Data Base of Products

Product	Price	TVC	Throughput per Unit (Tu)	Time on CCR (min)	Tu/Min on CCR
Normal	85	35	50	10	**10.00**
Soft	160	120	40	10	**4.00**
Hard	72	57	15	5	**3.00**

Table 8-9
Maximum Profit Mix
CCR Capacity = 2,400 Demand/CCR capacity = 116.7%

Product	Demand (Forecast)	Maximum Throughput Mix	Acum. Utiliz. of CCR %	Total Throughput per Product
Normal	120	120	50%	6,000
Soft	10	10	54.2%	400
Hard	300	220	100%	3,600

Total Throughput	9,700
Operating Expense	9,000
Net Profit	**700**

To produce all the demand for this new product we will need 100 minutes of the CCR. We therefore have to free 100 minutes from the CCR's current load, and since Hard is the product that contributes the least to the company's profitability,[90] we will stop producing 100 minutes of this product, which is equal to 20 fewer units. Thus, the maximum profit mix becomes: 120 Normal + 10 Soft + 220 Hard. Thus the company's total throughput is US$ 9,700. Since OE was not altered, we will have a NP of US$ 700 a week (an increase of US$ 100).

Yet, even though the profit increased this approach did not show the best way. If we produce Smooth instead of Soft, the NP would be even bigger, even though Soft has a greater Tu/minute of the CCR.

[90] If we reduced the supply of Normal the introduction of any of the new products would decrease the financial results as both of them have a smaller throughput/time on the CCR than Normal.

Table 8-10
Data Base of Products

Product	Price	TVC	Throughput per Unit (Tu)	Time on CCR (min)	Tu/Min on CCR
Normal	85	35	50	10	**10.00**
Smooth	235	165	70	20	**3.50**
Hard	72	57	15	5	**3.00**

The maximum profit with Smooth is:

Table 8-11
Maximum Profit Mix
CCR Capacity = 2,400 Demand/CCR capacity = 129.2%

Product	Demand (Forecast)	Maximum Throughput Mix	Acum. Utiliz. of CCR %	Total Throughput per Product
Normal	120	120	50%	6,000
Smooth	20	20	66.7%	1,400
Hard	300	160	100%	2,400

Total Throughput	9,800
Operating Expense	9,000
Net Profit	**800**

The NP is US$ 200 higher than before any new product was introduced, and US$ 100 higher than with Soft. How can this happen? What happened is that all of Soft's demand uses only 100 minutes of the CCR, while all of product Smooth's demand uses 400 minutes.

If I choose to produce Soft, I am changing 100 minutes of Hard for 100 minutes of Soft. The difference between these products' Tu/minute of CCR is US$ 1, these means that for every minute that I stop producing Hard to produce Soft I am increasing the company's throughput by US$ 1. Thus, this exchange of 100 minutes of Hard for 100 minutes of Soft increases the total throughput by US$ 100.

However, if we produced Smooth, we would be exchanging 400 minutes of Hard for 400 minutes of Smooth. The difference between these products' Tu/minute of CCR is US$ 0.50, which means that for each minute that I stop producing Hard to produce Smooth I am increasing the company's throughput by US$ 0.50. Thus, this exchange of 400 minutes of Hard for 400 minutes of Smooth increases the total throughput by US$ 200. This shows that, under these conditions, producing Smooth is more profitable for the company.

We want to maximize the company's throughput, and to do so we need to use the CCR's time wisely. The Tu/minute of CCR is a measurement that shows us the relative contribution of each product to the company's profitability. However, as this case showed, under certain conditions, this relative contribution is not enough for us to make a decision; we also need to know the absolute contribution of each product to the company's throughput. This is a special case because we have to decide between launching to new products. Therefore we need to calculate the impact of launching each product, and then compare them. Here we need to calculate the difference between the Tu/minute of CCR of the two products in relation to the product being substituted, and then multiply this difference by the minutes that are going to be substituted (as I did in the previous paragraph). Or we just simulate the company's results for both cases, and make a decision based on the profitability differences between the two alternatives.

Whenever the CCR is overloaded and we have to increase the production of a product or launch a new product we need to decide which products will be substituted and in what quantities. This example shows how this decision is crucial. According to this choice launching the new product may or may not increase the profitability. If the new product (or the one whose production we want to increase) is substituting a product that has a higher Tu/minute of CCR then the bottom line will deteriorate, and vice-versa.

8.3. Setup

Up until now, to calculate the throughput per time of CCR we have not considered the setup time. There is a good reason for this. The CCR's time is too precious for the company because it establishes the company's maximum production. This is why the company should strive to eliminate the setup time (and not try to create complicated methods that take the setup time into consideration). To reduce the setup time we have the JIT techniques, which allow for great reductions of this time. We should not disperse our efforts by trying to use these techniques on every resource; we should focus them, especially on the CCR, where the setup time most jeopardizes the company's performance.[91]

Any method that takes into account the setup time will contain errors. However, while the company still has high setup times on its CCR, we can take them into account. What complicates this analysis is that in the calculation of the Tu/time of CCR we need to consider the setup time that each product will use of the CCR. Nevertheless, the setup time that each product will use depends on the number of batches, and that is a managerial decision. This is the problem—a management decision will establish the Tu/time of CCR.

We need a forecast of the setup time each product will use of the CCR, and to find this we have various methods. Every method has its flaws, but the company should not lose too much time discussing this point, instead it should focus its efforts on reducing the setup times on the CCR!

One possibility is to use the historical average of the batch sizes for each product in the calculation of the Tu/time of CCR. If the time period analyzed is not very long, another option is to assume that we will produce every product in one batch, and the size of the batch is the product's total demand. Another way of approaching the setup time is to decide how many batches will be used and what size these batches will be in order to supply the demand for each product in the period analyzed.

No matter what method is used, the formula to find the Tu/time of the CCR (considering setups) is the following:

[91] The setup time on the CCR is an opportunity cost, that is, it makes the company loose throughput. We will better understand this point later on.

(Demand x Throughput per unit) / [(demand x minutes per part) + (No. of batches x setup time)]

8.4. Cost of Scrap

The Total Quality movement raised concerns about the quality of companies' products. Consequently many companies implemented process and quality controls. Yet, what the quality movement did not do was to make clear that we should not try to solve everything at the same time. Moreover, we do not have enough resources to do that.

Scrap is a great quality problem in many companies. There are some techniques of how to reduce scrap in a plant, but this is not the point in this book. What we will see is where it is more profitable to start reducing scrap.

The CCR's localization in the process flow is very important to this analysis. If the CCR is overloaded, reducing the scrap before or after the CCR will have very different effects.

When we have scrap of a part before the CCR the cost of this scrap[92] is equal to the cost of the raw material (if we can still recycle this raw material, the cost is even lower). But, if the scrap results after the part has been processed by the CCR, the cost will be different. As already mentioned, when the CCR is the system's constraint, any minute of its time that is wasted is a minute less in the company's throughput. Therefore, if there is scrap of parts that have been processed by the CCR, we will be wasting the time the CCR spent processing that part. The cost of this scrap will be a sum of the raw material cost plus the opportunity cost of having lost the CCR's processing time (loss of throughput). Since the opportunity cost of a minute on the CCR is equal to one minute of throughput of the company, the cost of the scrap of a part that has been processed on the CCR is considerably high. To illustrate this let us use the following example:

Company XYZ has a very simple plant, with 5 steps (figure 8-1), and its CCR is overloaded. The raw material enters the process at resource A, is processed in the shown sequence up to resource E, where the product is ready to be sold. The number in each step is the average capacity of each resource in parts/hour. This company

92 Poor quality has many negative effects on the company, like increasing WIP, increasing production lead-time, decreasing customer satisfaction, and so on. Here we will only take into account the more tangible costs.

sells only one product (X), with a price of US$ 100 and raw material cost of US$ 35, which results in a throughput of US$ 65. The company's resources work 8 hours a day, 22 days a month, which results in 176 hours a month.

Figure 8-1
XYZ plant

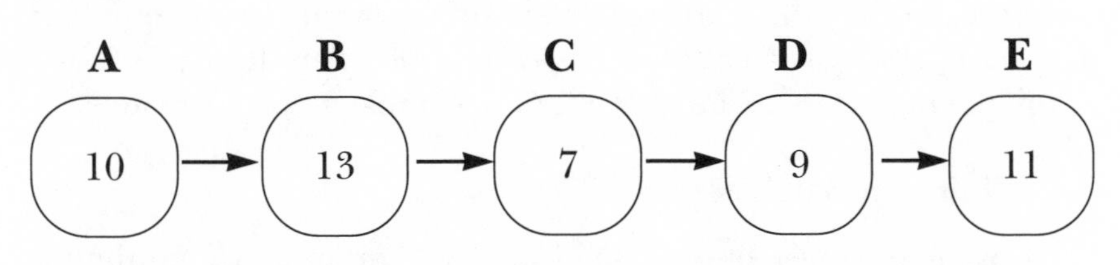

This plant's CCR is resource C, which limits the system's performance to 7 parts an hour. Before resource C the scrap is equal to 5%, which means that for every 100 parts that enter the plant, only 95 reach resource C with good quality. After resource C the scrap is also 5%.

Let us calculate the cost of these scraps.

If the company had no scrap it would be able to produce and sell 1,232 units a month (assuming 100% efficiency of the CCR). To do this it would use 1,232 units of raw material. This would generate a revenue of US$ 123,200 and a raw material cost of US$ 43,120, resulting in a total throughput of US$ 80,080.

However, given the current level of scrap, for the company to be able to produce the maximum possible it will have to feed the plant with more than 1,232 units of raw material. To use 100% of the CCR's time we will have to feed the plant with 1,297 units of raw material,[93] because of the 5% scrap between the initial operation and the CCR. Even by maintaining the CCR working 100% of its time the company will not be able to produce and sell 1,232 units of X, because of the 5% scrap between the CCR and the last operation. Maximum production will be 1,170 units.[94]

To calculate the cost of this scrap let us use two simulations, in which we eliminate the scrap from the plant, one piece at a time, and calculate the impact on the company's performance.

If we eliminate the scrap before the CCR we will not need to feed

[93] 1,232 / 0.95 = 1,296.84
[94] 1,232 * 0.95 = 1,170.40

the plant with 1,297 units, but only with 1,232. This increases Net Profit by US$ 2,275 a month.

If we eliminate the scrap after the CCR, we will be able to sell 1,232 units of X, which will generate an extra sales of US$ 6,200 (62 more units sold). Since the raw material of this extra 62 units were already paid for (they were scrap), this elimination of the scrap after the CCR will increase Net Profit by US$ 6,200. This is more than 2.5 times greater than the increase in Net Profit generated by eliminating the scrap before the CCR (which was also 5%). This illustrates, once again, the importance of the CCR in the company's performance.

8.5. Minimum Batch Size

Most companies have a sales policy that imposes minimum batches on their clients. What is the reasoning behind this policy?

The search for high local efficiencies is what establishes a minimum batch policy. A company does not want to make setups on its resources just to produce a few parts.

Still, as we have seen, this preoccupation is valid only if the setups have any impact on the company's CCR. Otherwise, a company may accept small batches, because this will increase its sales and will not have an impact on its OE (see the discussion about economic batch sizing in chapter 6). Even if the operation has an impact on the CCR, this will only affect the company's performance if it is overloaded.

In other words, the minimum batch policy is based on the cost world; it is based on the search for high local efficiencies. Many companies lose sales because of this policy, and this shows that the policy itself might be a constraint. This is an example of what I have already discussed, that in most companies the constraints are not physical (a machine), rather they are policy constraints. This example also shows another consequence of using cost accounting as a basis for decision-making.

What we need to keep in mind is that even if we do not explicitly use cost accounting, its concepts are so ingrained that we use them without noticing.

8.6. More Than One CCR

Some plants might have more than one CCR. This occurs when the company sells various products that are processed by different resources in some part of the process. Given this scenario the company might have more than one CCR.

To make decisions when the company has more than one CCR we need one statement for each CCR. We have to calculate the throughput that goes through each CCR, and then add them up to get the company's total throughput. From this amount we subtract the company's OE and get the NP.

Let us see a simple example of this type of case. A company has two CCRs. Four products go through the first one and three through the second, as shown in the statements below:

Table 8-12
Data Base of Products—CCR 1

Product	Price	TVC	Throughput per Unit (Tu)	Time on CCR (min)	Tu/Min on CCR
A	72	49.5	22.5	5	**4.50**
B	35	14.5	20.5	5	**4.10**
C	102	43.05	58.95	15	**3.93**
D	57	24	33	15	**2.20**

Table 8-13
Data Base of Products—CCR 2

Product	Price	TVC	Throughput per Unit (Tu)	Time on CCR (min)	Tu/Min on CCR
E	110	58	52	10	**5.2**
F	70	40.6	29.4	7	**4.2**
G	86	45.5	40.5	15	**2.7**

Table 8-14
Forecast of Results—Maximum Profit Mix/Marketing Mix—CCR 1
CCR capacity = 2,400 Demand/CCR capacity = 126.5%

Product	Demand (Forecast)	Maximum Throughput Mix	Sales Mix	Acum. Utiliz. of CCR %		Total Throughput per Product	
A	120	120	120	25.0%	25.0%	2,700	2,700
B	232	232	231	73.3%	73.1%	4,756	4,735.5
C	50	42	21	100%	86.3%	2,475.9	1,237.95
D	35	0	22	100%	100%	0	726

Throughput CCR 1 9,932.9 9,399.45

Table 8-15
Forecast of Results—Maximum Profit Mix/Marketing Mix—CCR 2
CCR capacity = 2,400 Demand/CCR capacity = 200%

Product	Demand (Forecast)	Maximum Throughput Mix	Sales Mix	Acum. Utiliz. of CCR %		Total Throughput per Product	
E	130	130	80	54.2%	33.3%	6,760	4,160
F	50	50	35	68.8%	43.5%	1,470	1,029
G	210	50	90	100%	100%	2,025	3,645

Throughput CCR 2 10,255 8,834

Throughput CCR 1	9,931.9	9,399.45
Throughput CCR 2	10,255	8,834
Total Throughput	20,186.9	18,233.45
Operating Expense	17,500	17,500
Net Profit	2,686.9	**733.45**

NP difference 1,953.45

As we can see, all we need to do is separate the calculation of the throughputs per CCR and then add them up to calculate the company's OE.

The above example assumes that all the company's products go through only one CCR. In some cases there might be one CCR that feeds another CCR, which means that we have two weakest links on the same chain. In fact one is the weakest link but the capacity of the other link is so close to the weakest link's capacity that the statistical fluctuation turns them into interactive constraints, something we should avoid.[95]

In this chapter we saw other examples of how to make decisions according to TOC. As you have no doubted noted, decisions according to TOC are very different from (often in conflict with) the decisions we are used to making. Even though they are very different, they make sense. In reality, our intuition is much more in line with TOC than with cost accounting.

In the previous chapters we saw that we should not use product costs to make good decisions. We saw that if we use product costs we will make irrational decisions. This is not something that is easy for us to accept, since all of our training, in all of the company's areas (production, marketing, engineering, etc.) are based on this concept. Even if my explanation of this subject were rigorously logical you would most likely, be skeptical. You might have asked questions like: "Is product costing such a wrong concept? Is it possible that we are all using such a misguided concept?"

These are very natural questions. After all almost all companies use product costs to make decisions. Even some successful companies. How can we explain this?

The next chapter will deal with this topic.

[95] See appendix.

9
Paradigm Shift in Management Accounting

There are many methodologies recommended today as solutions for the lack of relevance in traditional cost accounting: Activity-Based Costing (ABC), Activity-Based Management (ABM), Strategic Cost Management (SCM), for example. Use of these methodologies is often presented as a paradigm shift, when they are in fact extensions of the current paradigm. In chapter 5 we compared TOC with ABC. I decided to use ABC in this comparison because it is considered by many to be the best alternative to traditional cost accounting, although I stated that this choice was not that significant because all these "new" cost accounting methodologies are really based on the same paradigm. To make this more clear let us first understand what a paradigm is, and then when can see what a paradigm shift is and how it occurs.

According to economist Adam Smith, a paradigm is: "A shared set of assumptions. The paradigm is the way we perceive the world; water to the fish. The paradigm explains the world to us and helps us to predict its behavior."[96] He also says that "When we are in the middle of the paradigm, it is hard to imagine any other paradigm."[97]

For Barker a paradigm is "a set of rules and regulations (written or unwritten) that does two things: (1) it establishes or defines boundaries; and (2) it tells you how to behave inside the boundaries in order to be successful."[98]

Given these definitions we can conclude that a paradigm shift is a change in the basic assumptions of the field in question, a change in the rules of the game, a new set of rules. Different paradigms vary significantly in their basic assumptions.

[96] BARKER, Joel Arthur. *Paradigms, the Business of Discovering the Future.* New York: Harper Business, 1993, p. 31.
[97] *Ibid.*, p. 31.
[98] *Ibid.*, p. 32.

Since a paradigm shift is the creation of a new set of rules (abandoning the majority of the old rules), and "When we are in the middle of the paradigm, it is hard to imagine any other paradigm,"[99] people who adhere to the current paradigm will not be the ones who will change the paradigm. In fact, they will be against any paradigm shift.

Therefore, a paradigm shift is not something smooth, as the title of Kuhn's book suggests.[100] A paradigm shift is a revolution. Who generally makes revolutions? Certainly not the people that are in power, not these people that practice the current paradigm.

Let us analyze here the two categories of "revolutionaries" identified by Kuhn:

1. A young man who just finished training. He has studied the paradigm, but did not put it in practice.
2. An older person changing areas. Most likely the person is an expert in another area and, for some reason, decided to change completely.

> Let's stop for a minute to examine what advantages these two categories of people have in common. First, they both share **operational naiveté** about the fields they have just entered. They do not understand many of the subtler aspects of the paradigm community they want to be part of. Second, they do not know what **cannot** be done. Why is that an advantage? Very simply, if you do not know you cannot achieve something, sometimes you do it . . . the great advantage these people have is a special kind of ignorance. . . . They ask 'dumb' questions . . . They do not realize they shouldn't challenge the present practices because they haven't learned those prohibitions yet.[101]

Because they are either unaware or fresh in the face of the current paradigm revolutionaries do not possess a sense of propriety over it and therefore have a greater tendency to question it, to innovate. Revolutionaries do not have much to lose by defending a new

[99] BARKER, J. A. *Paradigms* . . . p. 31.
[100] KUHN, Thomas S. *The Structure of Scientific Revolutions*. Second Edition, enlarged. Chicago: The University of Chicago Press, 1970. Kuhn was a pioneer in the study of paradigms.
[101] BARKER, J. A. *Paradigms* . . . p. 59.

theory, while practitioners of the current paradigm have a lot to lose.

Let us spend a moment analyzing the fact that revolutionaries are not part of the paradigm in question. "These people are bringing you your future. And yet, as outsiders, what is their credibility? Zero, right? They cannot begin to understand what you are doing and yet here they are telling you to change the fundamentals of what you are so good at!"[102]

As we have just seen, the most famous people in their fields are against a paradigm shift. Nothing could be more natural. They built their careers (many times brilliant ones) a top the current paradigm, and it is natural that they do not accept the opinion of laymen.

When the defenders of a current paradigm talk about a revolutionary, they usually state that that person does not know anything of the area in question. The truth is that the revolutionaries do not have a deep understanding of the current paradigm; they are trying to bring a new paradigm to the area.

"New paradigms put everyone practicing the old paradigm at great risk. The higher one's position, the greater the risk. The better you are at your paradigm, the more you have invested in it, the more you have to lose by changing paradigms."[103]

However, I do not want to give the impression that the defenders of a prevailing paradigm are the villains of scientific evolution. If there were no resistance to new paradigms, knowledge would not evolve. If everyone changed constantly, we would not develop a theory to its fullest potential.

> The transfer of allegiance from paradigm to paradigm is a conversion experience that cannot be forced. . . . The source of resistance is the assurance that the older paradigm will ultimately solve all its problems, that nature can be shoved into the box the paradigm provides. Inevitably, at times of revolution, that assurance seems stubborn and pig-headed as indeed it sometimes becomes. But it is also something more. That same assurance is what makes normal or puzzle-solving science possible. And it is only through normal science that the professional community of scientists succeeds, first, in exploiting the potential scope and precision of

[102] *Ibid.,* p. 56.
[103] *Ibid.,* p. 69.

> the older paradigm and, then, in isolating the difficulty through the study of which a new paradigm may emerge.[104]

Why do paradigm shifts eventually occur, whether we want them to happen or not? This happens because paradigms become obsolete. Let us analyze, briefly, the evolution of a methodology.

Why do we create a new solution for something? Obviously, in order to eliminate problems and better our lives, we are trying to change reality. A new methodology is based on the problems we currently encounter on our daily lives. If the methodology were successfully implemented what would happen? Our reality would change. If we do not change reality, we will not improve our performance. I am not saying that all change necessarily leads to improvement, but that without change there can be no improvement.

Assuming that we have changed our reality, what happens to the methodology (policies) we created to change reality? Let us analyze this a little more carefully. We created the methodology based on a reality that we intend to change. We are effective and succeed in changing reality, therefore we change some, or all, the assumptions that were the basis of the new methodology. What can we conclude from this? That the new methodology will become obsolete, and the more effective it is, that is, the faster and better it changes reality, the faster it will become obsolete!

We are using a methodology that significantly altered reality. This methodology was primarily responsible for the significant improvement in our performance, and because of that it is now obsolete. Yet we have the tendency to make extrapolations from the past, that is, to think that if something worked very well up until now then it will continue to work very well. In such a situation we will not be open to change. Often what happens is that we try to adapt a methodology in an attempt to continue improving without changing our basic assumptions. We use the following reasoning: "It worked so well up until now that we should not stop using it." We create new policies from this 'old' solution. We go against common sense. We end up turning the great solution from the past into the great problem of the present!

If a new solution changed the reality upon which it was based, this means that the assumptions upon which this solution was based might no longer be valid. This leads us to conclude that we should

[104] KUHN, T. S. *The Structure* . . . p. 152.

not think that if something worked in the past then it will continue to work in the future.

This reasoning leads us to the increasingly widespread belief that an organization needs to create an environment that favors a process of continuous improvement, where change is the policy.

9.2. The Paradigm of Cost Methodologies

Management Accounting's objective is to provide information for decision making, make a connection between managers' local actions and the company's profitability. With this objective in mind we can cite the basic assumptions behind traditional management accounting (cost accounting).

One assumption is that we need product costs to make decisions, and that allocation base provide good information, both of which assumes that the company's costs have a direct one-to-one link with some quantifiable variable.

However, the main assumption behind all this accounting is that the sum of local optima leads to global optimum; in other words, that we can divide the organization into many areas and manage them as if they were independent of each other. This assumption is still the base of the 'new' cost methodologies, an therefore are still based on the scientific management paradigm. "The global optimum is broken down into local, sublocal, individual, everlasting, under control optima, all answering to the logical absolute: the perfect organization."[105]

The mechanisms and measurements of these 'new' methodologies are basically the same as traditional cost accounting—the allocation of costs to products, the formation of product costs, local efficiency measures, etc. Defenders of the 'new' methodologies are primarily people who have been immersed in traditional cost accounting.

On the other hand, TOC has significantly different assumptions. There is no calculation of product costs, there is no allocation basis, the costs do not have a direct one-to-one link with any quantifiable variable and, most of all, the sum of local optima does not lead to global optimum. TOC breaks the scientific management paradigm, by viewing the company as an organism, wherein a system of local optima is not a optimal system, but a very inefficient system. Its creator, Eliyahu Goldratt, is a physicist, someone who, like Kuhn's defi-

[105] LORINO, P. *O Economista* . . . p. 63, my translation.

nition of a revolutionary, is not from the field in question. TOC's methodology for management accounting was, and still is, openly criticized by most people who adhere to management accounting's current paradigm.

These three things: 1. Not sharing basic assumptions with the current paradigm; 2. Being criticized and resisted by the practitioners of the current paradigm and; 3. Having been created by someone from outside of the field, are what shows TOC to be a paradigm shift in management accounting. These same three characteristics do not apply to the other 'new' methodologies, and this confirms what I argued previously: that the other methodologies are only new articulations on top of the current paradigm.

9.3. Conclusion

In my view, TOC (and other theories) will lead to a great revolution in management, just like scientific management brought a century ago. They all have one thing in common: they advocate abandoning the scientific management paradigm for a new paradigm, one that views the company as a system.

As I stated in the introduction, scientific management cannot continue to be the basis for our management principles, because it is obsolete. "Classical management theory and scientific management were each pioneered and sold to managers as the one best way to organize'. . . . And indeed if we look closely, we find that their management principles often lie at the basis of many modern organizational problems."[106]

In my view, cost accounting is obsolete, but its obsolescence does not come from the way we use it, but from the concept of cost accounting itself. Cost accounting's loss of relevance did not occur because it allocated costs using direct labor as a basis, but because it allocated costs. This implies that not only traditional cost accounting but also activity-based costing and any other methodologies that are based on local optima are obsolete.[107]

[106] MORGAN, Gareth. *Images of Organization.* Newbury Park: Sage Publications, 1986, p. 33.

[107] These costing methodologies are obsolete but still need to be used for external purposes, for the IRS, for example. Nevertheless, even to obey the law we do not need the more complex (and extremely expensive) cost accounting procedures: Conventional cost accounting is sufficient. In other words, no company should implement the 'new' cost accounting methodologies.

At the end of the previous chapter we asked why most companies were still using such misguided concept. I hope that this chapter has helped you to answer that question. Cost accounting was very helpful in the past, which is why it is still used in the present. However, because it was so useful, it changed reality, which made it obsolete. Today, cost accounting mentality is one of the major constraints for the majority of companies. What happened is that the great solution of the past became the great problem of the present, because we have not fully understood that its time has passed.

Our resistance to abandoning cost accounting comes from its great utility in the past. Still, what you must realize is that what keeps companies that use cost accounting competitive is the fact that their competitors also use cost accounting.

10
Cost World v. Throughput World

In chapter 3 we saw the formulae for NP and ROI, which are the following:

NP = T - OE
ROI = (T-OE)/I

The NP formula gives us the impression that throughput and OE have the same importance. To increase NP by US$ 1 you can increase T by US$ 1 or decrease OE by US$ 1. If we have this impression, and because OE is more tangible - the company has more direct control over OE than over T - OE will be considered the most important measurement. This means we will direct most of our efforts towards reducing OE. This impression derives from the cost accounting paradigm, from the cost world.

We have seen that in this paradigm the main measurement is OE - costs. Now we need to know which one of the two remaining measures is more important, T or I. Investment only appears in one of the formulae, which gives us the impression that it only affects the company's ROI. Therefore T is more important because it has a direct influence on both formulae.

Thus, the scale of priorities in the cost world is:
First, OE; second, T and; third, I.

This means that the company's managers will prioritize cost reductions, then increase throughput and lastly investment reductions.

However, if we want to commence a process of ongoing improvement where should we concentrate? If the company's objective is to increase its profitability, where should we concentrate, on reducing costs or on increasing throughput or on reducing investment?

What is the limit when reducing costs or investment? Zero. We cannot reduce either below zero, therefore this does not allow for continuous improvement. Moreover, if this is the main measurement what is the end goal? Closing the company, so we will not have any more costs!

Now, what is the limit when increasing throughput? Infinite, and this allows for continuous improvement. If this is the main measurement what is the end goal? Having unending profitability! Therefore, throughput should be the main measurement, because the company was not created to save costs, but to make money.

Throughput is the only way out. It should be the main measurement, the measurement that directs the managers' actions and decisions. TQM has already advocated this by demanding improvements in quality, in delivery time, in customer services, etc. Why? It was certainly not to reduce costs,[108] but to increase throughput.

Therefore, throughput should be the first measurement in the scale of priorities. Which one should come next, OE or I? OE influences NP and ROI directly. In the west, we know that investment also influences OE (the greater the inventory the higher the costs). But what we did not acknowledge explicitly is that WIP and finished good inventories have great impact on the company's throughput. This is what JIT showed us. The greater the WIP the longer the production lead-time, the longer the response time to the market, the worse the quality, etc. All of this has great impact on the company's sales volume in both the short and long-run.[109] This is so important that investment should be the second measurement in our scale of priorities.

In the west we are so immersed in the cost world that when we first came in contact with the TQM and JIT movements we only thought about how they could help us reduce our costs, and completely ignored the real goal of these movements, which is to increase sales (throughput), and hence conquer more market share.

The scale of priorities in the throughput world is:

First, T; second, I and; third, OE.

Completely different from the current scale of priorities.

Again, let us use the chain analogy to compare these two perceptions—the cost world and the throughput world.

[108] These attitudes reduce costs, but this was not the main cause for the Japanese to do them, they were a positive side-effect.

[109] To have a better understanding of the impact of WIP on the company's competitiveness read *The Race.*

The cost world uses the company's costs as its main measurement, measured by the sum of each activity's costs. We can reduce a company's cost at any link: a cost reduction at any link reduces the company's costs. Comparing that to a chain, it is as if the main measurement is the chain's weight. This creates the impression that an improvement in any link is an improvement in the system as a whole. If we reduce the weight of a link by 50 grams, we will be reducing the weight of the whole chain by 50 grams. This is the main assumption of the cost world - that the sum of local optima leads to global optimum. As long as we consider cost reduction to be the main road to the company's goal, we will conclude that any improvement in any link constitutes an improvement in the entire chain.

TOC's uses the company's throughput as its main measurement. Comparing this to a chain it is as if the main measurement is the chain's strength. As a result most of the improvements in most of the links do not improve the chain as a whole. If we increase the strength of any link we will not necessarily be increasing the chain's strength. To do that we need to increase the strength of the weakest link. This is the basic assumption of the throughput world - that most of the local improvements do not improve the chain's performance. If we consider the increase in throughput to be the main road to the company's goal, we will conclude that any local improvement is not a global improvement.

Let us examine more closely why throughput should be the main measurement. To this end, let us leave aside for a moment systems whose goal is to make money and let us analyze a not-for-profit school, whose goal is to educate. This school uses the same measurements of investment and operating expense as a system whose goal is to make money, and these two measurements are still monetary measurements. But what about throughput? Is it also monetary? No, throughput has to be measured according to the system's goal. If the goal is to educate then the measurement has to be related to the levels of education, for example, how many students graduate per year and what the difference is in their level of education, comparing this when they enrolled to when they graduate. We do not calculate the school's NP because throughput is measured in level of education and OE is a monetary measurement. OE and investment are necessary conditions to obtain throughput, but the goal is to increase throughput.

In a system where the goal is to make money now and in the future, it is coincidental that the three measurements are monetary.

Therefore we can calculate NP, but we should not forget that the most important measurement is throughput. This is the measurement that will always be established according to the system's goal, whatever the goal is. The throughput measures what we want the organization to do in the first place, while OE and investment are conditions that enable us to move towards that goal.

"If a process of ongoing improvement is what we are after, which one of the three avenues of throughput, inventory, or operating expense is more promising? If we just think for a minute the answer becomes crystal clear. Both inventory and operating expense we strive to decrease. Thus, both of them offer only a limited opportunity for ongoing improvement. They are both limited by zero. This is not the case with the third measurement, throughput. We strive to increase throughput. Throughput does not have any intrinsic limitation; throughput must be the cornerstone of any process of ongoing improvement. It must be first on the scale of importance."[110]

"What actually happened when we deposed operating expense as king of the mountain, and replaced it with throughput? The realization of the magnitude of the change required is just now starting to emerge. It is actually the switch from viewing our organizations as systems of independent variables to viewing them as systems of dependent variables. . . . Ask yourself, 'How many outlets of operating expense exist in a company?' Every worker is an outlet, every engineer, salesman, clerk, or manager is an outlet of operating expense. Every bit of scrap, every place where we consume energy is an outlet of operating expense. This is the 'cost world'.

Of course, not everything is important to the same degree. Some things are more important than others. Even in the cost world, we recognize the Pareto principle, the 20-80 rule. Twenty percent of the variables are responsible for 80 percent of the end result. But this rule is statistically correct only when we are dealing with a system of independent variables. The "cost world" gives the perception that our organization is actually such a system-that the outlets of operating expense are hardly connected. Money leaks from many small and big holes.

Now, look at the picture when throughput becomes dominant in our perception. Many functions have to carry out, in synch, many tasks, until a sale is realized, until throughput is gained. The 'throughput world' is a world of dependent variables."[111]

[110] GOLDRATT, E. *The Haystack* . . . p. 49.
[111] *Ibid.,* p. 52.

For a company to obtain throughput it must project, produce, sell, distribute, etc. its products. All the company's activities have to take place in a pre-determined sequence. If any of the departments fail, the company will not be able to obtain throughput.

Therefore, when we view throughput as the main measurement, this makes us see the company as a chain, formed by many interdependent links, and this leads us in turn to the assumption that most of the local improvements in most of the links do not improve the chain's performance. Thus, managers from all areas are forced to see the company as a system, which is different from the cost world mentality that forces managers to view each link as independent.

TQM and JIT also have their problems with cost accounting. "TQM was irritated . . . by the fact that the investment in improving quality, which is done for the sake of the very important throughput gains, has to be justified by a much less important cost consideration. They simply solved their problem by shoving aside the financial measurements, stating that 'Quality is Job One.' JIT has done basically the same thing. When I met Dr. Ohno, the inventor of KANBAN, the JIT system of Toyota, he told me that cost accounting was one thing that he had to fight against all his life. It was not enough to chase out the cost accountants from the plants, the problem was to chase cost accounting from my people's minds.'"[112] This change in mentality is the change from the cost world to the throughput world.

The reduction of OE is the main goal of the cost world. According to this line of reasoning a process of ongoing improvements is impossible. This is due to two factors. We have already discussed the fact that if the focus is reducing costs then there is a limit - we cannot reduce below zero. In reality we do not get even near zero, therefore we cannot improve continuously. The second factor is related to the kind of costs we cut.

Most of us agree that companies need to embark on a process of ongoing improvement in order to compete. We also agree that to enter a process of ongoing improvements we need to motivate people. The quality movements have shown this.

To cut costs we need to "attack" an OE item that has great impact on total costs. What item of cost today is responsible for most of expenses? Payroll. Our conclusion: to improve continuously we must

[112] *Ibid.*, p. 55

both fire and motivate people at the same time! The road the cost world takes us down is a dead end.

In the introduction I stated TOC was in line with other theories, that these were also based on the same systemic paradigm, that Goldratt was not alone. However, some of these other theories, like TQM and JIT, have not completely abandoned the cost world mentality. They are also based on the systemic paradigm, but they do not include an effective process of ongoing improvement because they still stimulate the improvement of all the system's links (example: setup reduction on all machines). This is one of the main reasons why TQM takes so long to produce results: it does not focus, it does not identify the constraint.

I have already stated that TQM and JIT established the prioritization of the three measurements.

Goldratt's process of ongoing improvement makes TOC complementary to TQM and JIT. This process is comprised of the five steps we saw in chapter 3:

1. Identify the system's Constraint(s).
2. Exploit the Constraint(s).
3. Subordinate everything to the above decision.
4. Elevate the Constraint(s).
5. If a constraint is broken go back to Step 1, but do not let inertia become a system's constraint.

These steps guarantee continuous improvements, and they are based on throughput as the main measurement. Because there is no limit to how much throughput can increase, a process of ongoing improvement is possible. If a company wants to improve continuously it has to identify and explore its constraints. If you agree that the above process is logical, then a methodology that does not follow this process cannot be correct.

In TOC throughput is the main measurement. The main concern for managers should be to increase throughput. To increase throughput we have to bear in mind that the company's OE represents how much it pays to have its capabilities available. What I mean by capability is everything the company's resources can produce, not only what it produces today, but everything it can produce if it wants to, without needing to significantly increase OE and investment.

With this definition in mind, we can now answer the following question: what is the company's share of the global market, taking its capabilities into account? Extremely low, near 0%! This means that there is enough market for the company to increase its sales, and what we need to do is to capture this market. From this we can conclude that the market is not a constraint for the vast majority of companies - what blocks these companies from capturing the market are erroneous marketing policies, which, in most cases, are based on the 'cost world' mentality.[113]

What a company has to see is the potential of its capabilities. If a company explores these capabilities it will significantly increase its throughput without significantly increasing its OE and investment. To explore its available capabilities without increasing OE and investment a company has to know where its constraints are, to know where it has flexibility to increase the production volume and the product variety. The company's long-run should be based on these concepts.

10.1. The Use of Cost Accounting and TOC and Their Impact on the Company

Let us now see what happens when managers have the throughput world perception and when they have the cost world perception. Managers' perceptions of how to improve a company's performance are very important, because what controls changes in the organizations are its managers' actions and decisions, and what controls the managers' actions and decisions are their perceptions.

10.1.1. Perception of Value for the Company's Products

The fact that we use product costs to make decisions also results in some unforeseen consequences. When we have a product cost figure, we create a perception within the company that one fair price exits for a product. This fair price is the total of the costs to project, produce, distribute, sell, etc. the product plus a reasonable profit margin.

But we all know, at least intuitively, that the market's perception of value is associated with the benefits the product brings, and these benefits have no relationship to the product's cost, which is the producer's perception of value. Moreover, the market has several perceptions of value for the same product, and this creates great

[113] For more about this subject, see: *It's Not Luck* by E. Goldratt. Great Barrington: North River Press, 1994.

opportunities for increasing the company's profitability, and these opportunities are lost because of the perception of one fair price imposed by cost accounting.

If we charge US$ 40 for a product (cost + margin), the clients that perceive a lower value for this product will not buy it. On the other hand, the clients that perceive a higher value will only pay the US$ 40 charged. Therefore, we are losing volume with the clients who would buy the product at a lower price, and we are losing money with the clients who would pay more for the product. However, the most important thing is that even if the company's salesmen were to comprehend this, the cost mentality would not allow for an effective market segmentation.

"The basic difficulty with the idea that cost dollars, as incurred, attach like barnacles to the physical flow of materials . . .it is at odds with the actual process of valuation in a free competitive market. The customer does not buy a handful of classified and traced cost dollars; he buys a product, at prevailing market price. And the market price may be either above or below any calculated cost figure."[114]

I have already argued that most companies have a huge unexplored market, and what is keeping them from exploiting this potential are their marketing policies. These marketing policies are often derived from the cost world. The cost world mentality puts a straightjacket on the company's marketing strategies, because it offers a perception of value that is at odds with the market's perception of value. The company's marketing gets caught between two opposing forces. From one side it is obliged to increase sales and to do that it has to act according to the market's perceptions of value, and at the same time it is obliged to impose the company's perception of value on the market (product cost + margin). The cost world mentality, which created the product cost, ends up blocking many of the possible actions marketing could take to increase the company's throughput. Moreover, it also decreases the company's profitability because it does not indicate the most profitable products, and often finds some products highly unprofitable when in fact they are profitable, and vice-versa (as we saw in the RS example in chapter 5).

According to TOC management accounting's role is to verify whether the product will increase the company's profitability at the price established by the market. Hence there is a greater price flexibility in a TOC environment.

[114] JOHNSON and KAPLAN. *Relevance Lost* . . . Quoting William Patton, p. 139.

10.1.2. Impact on the Company's Strategies

Because the cost world gives equal importance to all a company's links, using cost world measurements require the collection of a sea of data. This demands a lot of time and money, which is often unfeasible for many companies, aside from simply increasing a company's costs.

Aside from the huge quantity of data needed, the cost world makes managers concentrate on reducing costs, and as we can reduce cost at any link of the system, the improvement efforts are dispersed across the entire organization, which leads to a less efficient process, and gives managers the impression that the company does not have enough resources to work effectively.

On the other hand, TOC focuses on very few links, which makes data collection much faster and cheaper. For a company to implement throughput accounting (as we saw in chapter 4) it does not require a lot of data. The greatest challenge when implementing TOC is not data collection, but the paradigm shift in people's minds.

However, there are other important issues. Where the information provided by each paradigm take the company is extremely important. And, as we have already seen, these two paradigms take the companies in very different directions.

> Managers reported that accounting statements prepared using TOC principles were much easier to understand than conventional accounting reports, and the effects of their actions on the accounting reports made more sense . . . Furthermore, some companies were taking advantage of the simplicity of TOC accounting to compile profit reports more frequently and on a more timely basis. These reports were being used to monitor the performance of the entire system.[115]

TA statements are much simpler to understand and use; they are much more in line with our intuition. Accordingly the company's decision-making process is more accessible, and the people who are supposed to make the decisions can understand and agree with what the company's information system is telling them. This facilitates communication between all departments and management account-

[115] NOREEN and SMITH and MACKEY. *The Theory* . . . p. xxiv.

ing, and we all know this does not happen with cost accounting and its complicated methodologies. To the contrary, very few people in an organization understand and/or agree with costing methodologies. If we want people to make decisions that take a company towards its goal we have to provide the means for them to do so.

"The mission of the measurements is one of decentralization of a decision process: directed to a global objective . . . , what are the local decision rules to be established to guarantee that the behavior is 'as coherent as possible' with the global objective?"[116]

As Goldratt says: "Tell me how you measure me and I will tell you how I will behave. If you measure me in an illogical way . . . do not complain about illogical behavior."[117] The cost world performance measurements generate many problems and conflicts in the work environment, and by making our work even harder this worsens the system's performance.

TOC's performance measurements, because they are simple and in line with the company's goal, also change the managers' behavior for better.

"TOC practitioners tend to put much more emphasis on increasing throughput and decreasing investment than on cutting costs. The basic reason is that really effective cost cutting programs almost inevitably will result in laying off employees, which creates a 'Catch-22' situation. Effective cost cutting programs such as TQM require the active and enthusiastic participation of employees. However, employees are unlikely to sustain interest in improvement programs if they observe that improvement leads to layoffs.

TOC managers prefer to find new business when improvement in processes exposes excess capacity or surplus resources. This preference for more business over cutting costs in TOC is not just wishful thinking. TOC supports greater diversity and greater volume in two ways:

- It improves operations so that the existing resources can handle greater diversity and volume.
- TOC accounting provides managers with more pricing flexibility because product costs are much lower under TOC accounting than conventional absorption costing.

[116] LORINO, P. *O Economista* . . . p. 120, my translation.
[117] GOLDRATT, E. *The Haystack* . . . p. 28.

In principle, there is a preference in TOC for entering new markets to increase throughput rather than for capturing more market share in existing markets. Such action avoids putting too many eggs in one basket and retaliation by competitors. Therefore, product diversity is encouraged in TOC, in marked contrast to activity-based costing (ABC). ABC usually discourages product diversity by shifting overhead costs to low-volume products, which then appear less profitable. In TOC, the default assumption is that overhead functions, like other nonconstraint work centers, can handle additional diversity without new resources. If they cannot, the overhead resources themselves become the constraint and can be dealt with using the usual TOC approaches. That is, improvement efforts can be focused on that part of overhead that is the constraint . . . At the sites we visited very few managers seemed concerned about problems of creeping overhead. For the most part, they seemed to be able to diversify and increase volume with relatively modest increases in overhead."[118]

"The product strategies of companies involved in TOC can differ dramatically from those of companies that use activity-based costing. TOC typically uncovers capacity and provides production flexibility that makes more variety possible in the company's product offerings. Products invariably appear more profitable in a TOC shop than in a shop where product margins are computed using full costs. Providing that a new product with positive throughput does not use the constraint, it will appear attractive. Therefore, products will tend to proliferate in a TOC environment. ABC, on the other hand, can lead easily to a decrease in product offerings. A switch from a conventional costing system with volume-related allocation bases to an ABC system with batch or product level cost pools will shift costs from high-volume to low-volume products. The usual result is a 'profitability map' that suggests low-volume products are losing money. If managers respond by dropping such products, the offerings of the company will shrink. Thus, TOC and ABC can have opposite effects on the variety of products offered by a company.

These differences in strategy can be traced back to differences in fundamental assumptions about the way costs behave."[119]

TOC stimulates product diversity. In today's competitive and

118 NOREEN and SMITH and MACKEY. *The Theory* . . . p. xxvi.
119 *Ibid.*, p. 143.

unstable market a company will be much safer if it has a presence in many market segments. As Johnson and Kaplan have argued:

"Increasingly, firms will compete based on economics of scope-the ability to produce a wide variety of products on the same manufacturing equipment . . ."[120] Nevertheless ABC (cost accounting) does not stimulate this type of behavior, as the research done by Noreen, Smith and Mackey has demonstrated.

By using TOC a company's management will start to look for new market opportunities, always keeping in mind the company's constraints and, therefore, understanding where the company can support a greater variety of products and a greater production volume without increasing OE. For TOC costs are not the most important factor. What is important is increasing throughput without increasing costs. This is how decisions should be made, which is why overhead does not increase in a TOC environment like it increases in other environments. If a company knows where it has flexibility, it will not need to increase its costs.[121]

[120] JOHNSON and KAPLAN. *Relevance Lost* . . . p. 217.

[121] I read the following quote on the Internet, which shows, humorously, the basic differences between the "cost world" and the "throughput world": "The pessimist thinks the glass is half empty. The optimistic thinks the glass is half full. The cost accountant thinks you have twice as much glass as you need. The throughput accountant thinks you have room for twice as much stuff."

11
Conclusion

In the cost world there is a constant search for high local efficiencies, with the objective of maximizing use of the company's resources/activities. Along this book I hope to have shown that the search for high efficiencies is harmful to a system, that is, it takes a system in the opposite direction of its goal.

Some defenders of the cost world have understood that: "JIT production policies also make traditional local efficiency measures such as individual worker output and machine uptime invalid."[122] But, in fact, the JIT policies have not made local efficiency measurements invalid, they have just shown they were not valid. But what defenders of cost accounting have not perceived is that not only are traditional local efficiency measurements not valid, but any measurement that stimulates high local efficiencies as well.

If cost world proponents perceived this, they could not support ABC (or any other cost world methodology). Cost drivers are local efficiency measurements that stimulate managers to optimize the use of every link in the chain (every activity), arguing that this will lead to global optimization. In reality, ABC tries to maximize the efficiency of all activities, and this, certainly, does not contribute to the system's performance.

Defenders of ABC argue that the information provided by the traditional cost accounting system may lead to bad decisions. "In some instances, the information reported by existing management accounting systems not only inhibited good decision making by managers, it might actually have encouraged bad decisions . . ."[123] Yet, as we have already seen, any methodology based on the cost world also leads to bad decisions, because it is not something new. It

[122] JOHNSON and KAPLAN. *Relevance Lost* . . . p. 223.
[123] *Ibid.,* p. 177.

is just a refinement of the traditional and obsolete cost accounting system.

This book has shown various undesirable effects caused by the cost world. Below are some of the effects.

- Too complicated, few people understand it and it is very expensive to implement;
- It is not in line with our intuition;
- It does not choose the best product mix, because it is not able to identify the products that most contribute to the company's profits;
- Its local efficiency measures cause increases in WIP, decrease in product quality, increase in production lead-time and worsen the company's customer service;
- Cost allocation to products stimulates management to increase WIP and finished goods inventories in order to artificially increase short-term profits;
- Some performance measurements are at odds with each other and with the company's goal;
- It suggests that some actions will improve the company's performance when in reality they worsen the performance;
- Blocks some actions that improve the company's performance;
- Creates the notion of cost per part that prevents the company from identifying improvements in its performance, thereby creating a perception of value that jeopardizes the company's marketing strategies;
- Ignores the existence of the system's constraints because it does not consider the company a system;
- It assumes that the company's costs always vary with changes in mix and/or with changes in production volume;
- Disperses efforts;
- Decreases product offerings to the market, again placing a straitjacket on the company's marketing policies (batch sizing, one fair price, and so on);
- Does not allow a process of ongoing improvement;
- Stimulates lay-offs and by doing so does not allow for the creation of a motivating work environment;
- Holds that local optima leads to global optimum; it is still based on concepts created a century ago and is therefore not a paradigm shift. It has not adapted to the new reality.

The search for local optimizations lead to poor system performance. Local performance measurements have to be subordinated to the company's goal; they cannot create local optimizations that take the company in the opposite direction of its goal. "An example of a system well optimized is a good orchestra. The players are not there to play solos as prima donnas, each one trying to catch the ear of the listener. They are there to support each other. Individually they need not be the best players in the country."[124]

Many people criticize TOC because it advocates focusing on throughput and, they argue, this leads people to ignore the company's costs, causing there increase. According to the research done by Noreen, Smith and Mackey costs in a TOC environment do not increase like they do in other environments. TOC does not advocate ignoring costs; it urges us to focus our attention not on reducing costs but on increasing throughput. The undesirable effects listed above confirm even more what we have already concluded - that managing according to the cost world increases the company's costs. Hence we can conclude that if we want to improve the company's performance by increasing its throughput and controlling its costs, we should not use cost accounting.

Today there is no way to provide relevant information by using allocations (whatever method used). Overhead represents the majority of a company's expenses, and this prevents allocation from providing useful information. You cannot forecast cost variation using allocation basis, and there is no need to try and do that. Moreover, there is no way of knowing the impact of a decision on a company's bottom line by looking at the cost of a local decision because the local cost has no relationship to its impact on the overall performance of the system.

A product's cost has no relationship with a company's bottom line. We have seen that we can increase a product's cost and by so doing increase a company's profit. We also saw that we can reduce a product's cost and by so doing reduce a company's profit. This will happen in the short or the long-run. There is no way that we can know the effect of a decision on the bottom line by looking at product cost. Cost accounting cannot provide trustworthy information because it is based on erroneous assumptions.

What we must keep in mind is that what really matters is not product cost but the impact of a decision regarding products on the

124 DEMING, W. *The New Economics*, p 96.

company's bottom line. To know that, we do not need to do any kind of allocation.

What we need to do is to manage the system's capacity, and we need to consider its capacity limits in our decisions. We also have to keep in mind that what limits the capacity of a system are its constraints, therefore to be able to better manage the system's capacity we need to identify and control its constraints. A company's OE represents the company's capacity - how much the company is paying to have its resources available. With this in mind we have to try and get the most out of these resources.

Many people still advocate the use of allocation methods through ABC (and other methods), forgetting that allocation was first designed to simplify the decision-making process. Now, in an effort to save allocation some people advocate an increase in the number of classifications which makes the decision-making process more complex and less effective.

Defenders of ABC argue that conventional accounting has lost relevance because it uses only one allocation base. But in fact, as we have seen, conventional cost accounting has lost relevance because it allocates costs. Consequently, ABC has also lost relevance. To change conventional cost accounting to ABC is like "rearranging deck chairs on the Titanic."[125]

For the reasons that we have seen here Goldratt has classified cost accounting, including ABC (and any other methodology based on the same paradigm), as the number one enemy of productivity.

If we agree with the view that a company is a system, and that a system will always have very few constraints, then all we can do is agree with Goldratt.

As we saw at the beginning of this book, we must change conventional management accounting. ABC changes very little of what we already have because it is still based on the principles of scientific management, and does not allow for a process of ongoing improvement. Scientific management was an excellent solution at the moment it was created. The view of the organization created by this movement was one of the main factors responsible for the great development companies had. But this movement significantly changed the reality for the companies, making itself obsolete in the process.

[125] JOHNSON, H. Thomas. "It's Time to Stop Overselling Activity-Based Concepts." *Management Accounting,* September, 1992 p. 30.

"The management instruments approach to the economic reality are in an advanced position in the mechanistic paradigm. Therefore, it is no surprise that they are, more and more, less adapted to the characteristics and needs of the contemporary company."[126] TOC's management accounting is much more in line with companies' current reality.

Cost accounting's core problem is its basis in local efficiency measurements, which demands cost allocation to products, and creates the figure of product costs. TOC has attacked this basis by questioning the notion that to make good decisions you need to allocate costs. In TOC, we do not calculate product costs. What we do is calculate the impact of each decision on the company's bottom line (on T, I and OE), and this is what matters. I believe that TOC principles solve management accounting's problems, by going from cost accounting to throughput accounting.

However, management accounting's problems are just a reflection of deeper organizational problems, which is why most management techniques/policies are based on obsolete principles. "Classical management theory and scientific management were each pioneered and sold to managers as the 'one best way to organize' . . . Now, we only have to look at the contemporary organizational scene to find that they were completely wrong on this score. And indeed, if we look closely, we find that their management principles often lie at the basis of many modern organizational problems."[127] What we have to understand is that our companies are systems, and to be able to manage them well we need to see and manage the connections between the system's various variables.

Our training is almost entirely based on an obsolete paradigm, which is why it is so hard for us to see any alternative. Even though a new theory makes sense, that is, even though it is logical and in line with our intuition, in reality we tend to apply what our training has taught us. This becomes even more evident when we see that most people who read *The Goal* consider it an excellent book—they think that the book is pure common sense. However, when we examine what these same people do in their day-to-day work, we see that they go against common sense. This also happens in business schools, many of which have already included *The Goal* as a pre-req-

[126] LORINO, P. *O Economista* . . . p. 83, my translation.
[127] MORGAN, G. *Images of* . . . p. 33.

uisite for students starting MBAs, yet during the course schools continue to teach the opposite of common sense.

The companies that first make this paradigm shift (completely) will certainly, have an enormous competitive advantage, because they will be competing with companies that do not know what they are doing (these still in the cost world.) Today what saves most companies is that their competitors also use product costs to make decisions. But some companies have changed and other are changing, and this gives them a great competitive advantage. History has shown us that those who innovate gain the lead, while those who do not change, are left behind.

In the beginning of the book I stated that many companies argue that the reasons for their lack of competitiveness lie in the outside world, that these reasons are out of their control. They blame the government, foreign exchange policies, interest rates, globalization, lack of a prepared workforce, and so on. However, as I have shown here managers still have a lot of room to improve their companies' performance without depending on external factors. We saw that a company's main constraints are policy constraints;[128] they are management practices that the managers impose. Thus, we are the ones that impose constraints on the company's performance!

On one hand, this can be bad, because it demands a great deal of self-criticism, but on the other hand it is excellent, because it opens a door for a significant increase in performance, because it means that an increase in performance depends only on us. What we need is courage to make this change, and this is not only true for managers but also for educators, who have the challenge of changing management courses ahead of them.

[128] The use of cost accounting is an example of a policy constraint.

Bibliography

BARKER, Joel Arthur. *Paradigms, the Business of Discovering the Future.* New York: Harper Business, 1993.

BERLINER and BRIMSON. *Cost Management for Today's Advanced Manufacturing.* Boston: Harvard Business School Press, 1988.

BRIMSON, James A. *Activity Accounting. An Activity-Based Costing Approach.* New York: John Wiley & Sons, 1991.

CHALOS, Peter. *Cost Management in the New Manufacturing Age.* Englewood Cliffs: Prentice Hall, 1992.

COGAN, Samuel. *Activity-Based Costing (ABC), a poderosa estratégia empresarial.* São Paulo: Pioneira, 1994.

COLLINS, James C. and PORRAS, Jerry I. *Built To Last—Successful Habits of Visionary Companies.* New York: Harper Business, 1994.

COOPER, Robin. "The Rise of Activity-Based Costing—Part One: What Is an Activity-Based Cost System?" *Journal of Cost Management for the Manufacturing Industry,* Summer 1988.

DARLINGTON, John et, al. "Throughput Accounting: The Garrett Automotive Experience." *Management Accounting,* April 1992.

DEMING, W. Edwards. *The New Economics.* Cambridge: Massachusetts Institute of Technology—Center for Advanced Engineering Study, 1997.

DETTMER, H. William. *Goldratt's Theory of Constraints: A System's Approach to Continuous Improvement.* Milwaukee: ASQC, Quality Press, 1996.

GALLOWAY, David and WALDRON, David. "Throughput Accounting, the Need for a New Language for Manufacturing." *Management Accounting* (UK), November 1988.

GALLOWAY, David and WALDRON, David. "Throughput Accounting, Part 2, Ranking Products Profitably." *Management Accounting* (UK), December 1988.

GALLOWAY, David and WALDRON, David. "Throughput Accounting, Part 3, A Better Way to Control Labour Costs." *Management Accounting* (UK), January 1989.

GALLOWAY, David and WALDRON, David. "Throughput Accounting, Part 4, Moving On to Complex Products." *Management Accounting* (UK) February 1989.

GOLDRATT, Eliyahu. *The Theory of Constraints Journal.* Volume 1, numbers 1 to 6. 1988: Avraham M. Goldratt institute.

GOLDRATT, Eliyahu. *Self-Learning Kit. Production the TOC Way.* Avraham Y. Goldratt Institute.

GOLDRATT, Eliyahu. *The Haystack Syndrome. Sifting Information Out of the Data Ocean.* Croton-on-Hudson: North River Press, 1990.

GOLDRATT, Eliyahu. *It's Not Luck.* Great Barrington: North River Press, 1994.

GOLDRATT, Eliyahu. *What is This Thing Called the Theory of Constraints and How Should It Be Implemented?* Croton-on-Hudson: North River Press, 1990.

GOLDRATT, Eliyahu M. and COX, Jeff. *The Goal.* Croton-on-Hudson: North River Press, 1986.

GOLDRATT, Eliyahu M. and FOX, Robert E. *The Race.* Croton-on-Hudson: North River Press, 1986.

HICKS, Douglas T. *Activity-Based Costing for Small and Mid-Sized Businesses: An Implementation Guide.* New York: John Wiley & Sons, 1992.

HORNGREN, Charles T. and FOSTER, George. *Cost Accounting, a Managerial Emphasis.* Englewood Cliffs: Prentice Hall International Editions, 1991.

JAYSON, Susan. "Goldratt & Fox: Revolutionizing the Factory Floor." *Management Accounting,* May 1987.

JOHNSON, H. Thomas. *Relevance Regained, from Top-Down to Bottom-Up Empowerment.* New York: The Free Press, 1992.

JOHNSON, H. Thomas. "It's Time to Stop Overselling Activity-Based Concepts." *Management Accounting,* September 1992.

JOHNSON, H. Thomas and KAPLAN, Robert S. Relevance Lost, the Rise and Fall of Management Accounting. Boston: Harvard Business School Press, 1991.

KAPLAN, Robert S. "The Evolution of Management Accounting." *Accounting Review*, July 1984.

KAPLAN, Robert S. "Yesterday's Accounting Undermines Production." *Harvard Business Review*, July/August 1984.

KAPLAN, Robert S. and COOPER, Robin. *Cost and Effect. Using Integrated Cost Systems to Drive Profitability and Performance.* Boston: Harvard Business School Press, 1998.

KUHN, Thomas S. *The Structure of Scientific Revolutions.* Chicago: The University of Chicago Press, 1970.

LEE, Terry Nels and PLENERT, Gerhard. "Optimizing Theory of Constraints When New Product Alternatives Exist." *Production and Inventory Management Journal*, Third Quarter 1993.

LORINO, Philippe. *O Economista e o Administrador, Elementos de Microeconomia para uma Nova Gestão.* São Paulo: Livraria Nobel, 1992.

LOW, James T. "Do We Really Need Product Costs? The Theory of Constraints Alternative." *Corporate Controller*, September/October, 1992.

MORGAN, Gareth. *Images of Organization.* Newbury Park: Sage Publications, 1986.

MORGAN, Malcolm and BORK, Hans. "Is ABC Really a Need, Not an Option?" *Management Accounting*, September 1993.

NAKAGAWA, Masayuki. *ABC—Custeio Baseado em Atividade.* São Paulo: Ed. Atlas, 1994.

NOREEN, Eric and SMITH, Debra and MACKEY, James T. *The Theory of Constraints and Its Implications for Management Accounting.* Great Barrington: North River Press, 1995.

O'GUIN, Michael C. *The Complete Guide to Activity-Based Costing.* New Jersey: Prentice Hall, 1991.

PATTEUSSON, Mike C. "The Product-Mix Decision: A Comparison of the Theory of Constraints and Labor-Based Management Accounting." *Production and Inventory Management Journal,* Third Quarter 1992.

SENGE, Peter. *The Fifth Discipline.* New York: Currency Doubleday, 1990.

SHERIDAN, John. "*Throughput with a Capital 'T'.*" *Industry Week,* March 1991.

UMBLE, Michael and SRIKANTH, Mokshagundam L. *Synchronous Manufacturing. Principles for World-Class Excellence.* Cincinnati: South-Western Publishing Co., 1990.

The ideas in this book are new and radically different from what most companies use today. I would like to know your opinion on these ideas. Do you agree? Disagree? Do you think that there are points where they can be improved?

My e-mail is as follows. :

corbett@cxpostal.com

Below are some TOC sites on the Internet:

www.northriverpress.com
www.corbett-toc.com
www.rogo.com
www.goldratt.com

Appendix—Balanced Capacity

One of the largest and most undesirable side effects of the cost world is the search for a plant with balanced capacities. Balanced capacity means that all the resources in the production process have the same average capacity. This search occurs because we want to optimize the utilization of all resources in a plant, because we think that if a resource is idle then we are loosing money (or at least that we have invested more money than necessary). We are under the erroneous assumption that if we utilize all resources to their maximum we will be making more money. In this appendix we will see why a plant with balanced capacities is not desirable[1].

Cost accounting mentality demands high local efficiencies, which means that all the company's resources should be constantly producing something. Since a plant is naturally unbalanced, it is not easy to achieve high efficiencies on all resources. One way of trying to solve this is to significantly increase the WIP. However, high WIP is not desirable, and the pressure to reduce costs ends up forcing many companies to try and create a plant with balanced capacities. In doing so, many think that they are making the best possible investment.

Two facts make a plant with balanced capacities an illusion and a danger for any company. They are: 1) Statistical fluctuations and; 2) Dependent events. Let us use a simple example to try to understand what these two phenomena do together.

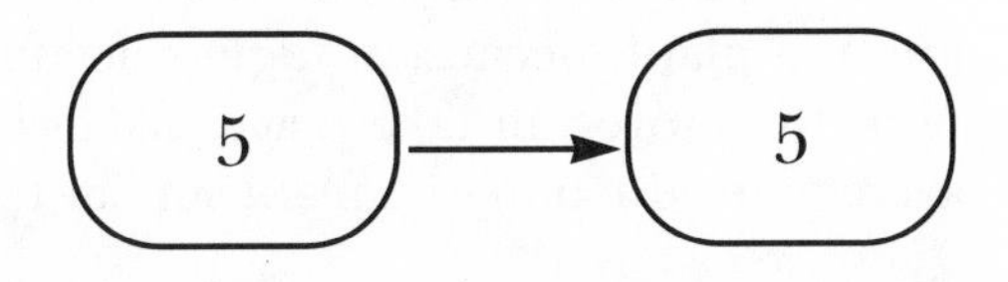

Figure 1—plant with 2 resources, each one with an average capacity of 5 parts/hour

[1] For more details, see: Chapter 3 of *Synchronous Manufacturing*, chapter 18 of *The Haystack Syndrome*; in addition, see the *TOC Journal*.

What is the average capacity of the plant? The first resource will be feeding the second resource with 5 parts/hour on average. How many parts/hour will the last resource be producing?

Let us use a binomial statistical distribution. We have two possible results, for both resources, of 4 or 6 parts/hour, with the same probability of occurrence. Thus, as I stated, the average capacity for each resource is 5 parts/hour. The question is: how much is the average capacity of the overall plant? Let us see what happens. Below we have a table showing the 4 possible occurrences and the final result that they impose on the plant.

Table 1

	1st Resource	2nd Resource	Result
	4	4	4
	4	6	4
	6	4	4
	6	6	6
Average	**5**	**5**	**4.5**

As we can see, the average of 5 parts/hour for each resource does not lead to an average of 5 parts/hour for the system as a whole. This is because the result of the first operation will be the starting point for the next operation. This plant only has 25% probability of producing 6 parts/hour, and at the same time it has 75% probability of producing 4 parts/hour. The first operation's statistical fluctuation accumulates and limits the production capacity of the second operation. The second resource will only produce 6 parts/hour if the first resource has produced 6 parts/hour. The dependency between the resources limits the statistical fluctuations upward, but not downwards. This means that the accumulation of statistical fluctuations limits the plant's production as a whole to the lowest individual result of the resources.

This phenomena has a greater impact the more resources there are in a plant, because a higher accumulation of statistical fluctuations therefore will take place. As an example of this let us see the average production of a plant similar to the one we just saw, but with 3 resources.

Table 2

	1st Resource	2nd Resource	3rd Resource	Result
	4	4	4	4
	4	6	4	4
	4	4	6	4
	4	6	6	4
	6	4	4	4
	6	6	4	4
	6	4	6	4
	6	6	6	6
Average	**5**	**5**	**5**	**4.25**

The more resources this plant has, the closer the average will get to 4 parts/hour, even though the individual average of all the resources is 5 parts/hour.

But, this is not all. What would happen if a plant had a balanced capacity? How many parts would enter the process every hour? 5 parts. How many parts would be produced every hour? Fewer than 5 parts. Therefore, the WIP increases if we maintain, or try to maintain, balanced capacities. Yet, this does not happen, because when the undesirable effects of balanced capacities start to multiply, management will quickly take measures, such as overtime, to unbalance the capacity. If management did not take this kind of action a plant with balanced capacities would go bankrupt.

"In a manufacturing plant, excess or unused capacity at a given resource is usually translated to mean excess cost. In the traditional cost-driven system, this excess cost is often the focus of cost reduction projects. In a vain attempt to minimize the cost at each process/resource, many manufacturing managers spend considerable time trying to balance the resource capacities in their plants. But as excess capacity is eliminated, the catch-up capability of the various resources disappears and the inevitable happens. The plant begins to fall further and further behind the production plan (gaps will form and grow) as work-in-process inventories increase and throughput lags. The blame for falling behind schedule is attributed to uncontrollable factors. Meanwhile, managers must resort to the use of overtime or other available means of increasing the capacity, in order to meet the production plan. Ironically, managers are soon paying a premium price for the capacity they previously worked so hard to trim."[2]

As we have seen, a plant with balanced capacities is not something desirable; it does not take the company towards its goal. Fortunately, a plant is naturally unbalanced, and our attempts to fight this phenomenon are what cause so many problems. A plant is like a chain: it always has very few weakest links.

To get the most out of a plant we need to make certain that all the plant's resources have at least a certain amount of capacity more than the CCR, so that the production flow is not interrupted causing the constraint to stop. This extra capacity is called protective capacity.

TOC classifies a resource's capacity in three categories:

1. **Productive capacity**—is the capacity that the company will use to process parts.
2. **Protective Capacity**—is the extra capacity needed on the nonconstraint resources for them not to interrupt the production flow, so that they do not stop the constraint.
3. **Idle capacity**—is the difference between the available capacity and the productive and protective capacities, i.e., what is leftover.

The size of the protective capacity depends on: 1) The level of statistical fluctuations, wherein the worse the quality of the process, the greatest the protective capacity will have to be; and 2) The size of the WIP, wherein the greater the WIP, the smaller the protective capacity can be. However, increasing the WIP will never be able to eliminate the need for protective capacity, because we would need an infinite WIP under this circumstance.

Thus we can conclude that to get the most of our investment (our plant), we need to make certain that we have only one weakest link, and that the other links have enough protective capacity to guarantee a smooth production flow. Most plant resources should have some idle time.

"To clarify it further, let's pretend that one of the feeding

[2] UMBLE, Michael and SRIKANTH, Mokshagundam L. *Synchronous Manufacturing. Principles for World-Class Excellence.* Cincinnati: South-Western Publishing Co., 1990, p. 63.

[3] That one of the resources that feeds the constraint has the same capacity that it has (my note).

resources does not have any spare capacity.[3] In such a case, what level of inventory do we need in front of the constraint to guarantee that we can always exploit it? Suppose that Murphy strikes this particular resource or any resource feeding it. The constraint will then have to eat into its inventory, and there is no way to replenish it. The level of protection is permanently lowered. Now Murphy strikes once more. Again the level of protective inventory drops. And on and on. . . . As long as we accept that Murphy does not go away, how much inven tory should we initially place in front of the constraint? Yes, if we do have another constraint in the chain—a resource having no spare capacity—we'd need infinite inventory to be able to exploit even one constraint.

A constraint. . . . must be shielded against Murphy by a combination of inventory placed right in front of it and the protective capacity of the resources feeding it. There is a trade-off between these two protection mechanisms. Less protective capacity in the feeding resources will require higher levels of inventory in front of the constraint. Otherwise, the constraint will be starved from time to time and throughput for the entire company will be lost. If one of the resources has zero protective capacity, the required inventory in front of the downstream constraint must be infinite.

Thus, if a chain has more than one weakest link, its strength will be considerably less than even the strength of each of its weakest links. Such a chain will be torn quickly by reality; systems containing interactive constraints are just transient in our fierce world.

We used to consider as waste any available capacity which is higher than what is strictly needed for production. Now, we realize that when we examine available capacity, we have to distinguish between three, rather than two, conceptual capacity segments. The first is productive capacity, the segment that we need for actual production to meet demand. The second segment is protective capa city, which is needed as a shield against Murphy. Only the constraint resource does not have protective capacity (remember-EXPLOIT). Any capacity remaining after we take into account productive and protective capacities is actually excess capacity."[4]

Protective capacity is not an unnecessary investment. On the contrary, it is absolutely necessary to adequate plant management.

[4] GOLDRATT, Eliyahu. *The Haystack Syndrome. Sifting Information Out of the Data Ocean.* Croton-on-Hudson: North River Press, 1990, p. 113.

The lack of protective capacity causes many problems, like increase in costs and lack of control of the plant's output.

"The previous discussion is not meant to be an argument for having great amounts of excess capacities. It is meant to emphasize that the focus on individual resource capacities encouraged by traditional cost systems is ill conceived."[5]

[5] UMBLE and SRIKANTH, *Synchronous Manufacturing* . . . p. 64.

On [illegible]
tragedies, the 4-year-old nephew she adopted burned

cynthia the force cooper

down her house accidentally (no one was seriously injured). But Old Pro, as Comets coach Van Chancellor dubbed her, missed only one game, the day after Perrot died. Says Cooper, "It's not the easy times that are the test, it's the tough times. I leaned on God to keep me strong, keep me motivated. My mom and Kim would have wanted me to stay strong and do just what the Comets did: win."

PHOTOGRAPH BY
ANNIE LEIBOVITZ

"I leaned on God last year," says three-time MVP Cooper.

She can cover 26.2 miles in one hour and 34 minutes—that's 32 minutes faster than the men's able-bodied marathon world record. She does it on carbon fiber wheels that glide along asphalt like blades on new ice. She's Jean Driscoll, seven-time winner of the Boston Marathon, two-time Olympic silver medalist in the 800-meter wheelchair exhibition. "I've gone jogging with presidents, and I've met queens," says Driscoll, 33. "It's not because of disability. It's because of ability."

Driscoll has won seven Boston Marathons.

Born with spina bifida, Driscoll walked with crutches for the first years of her life but was forced to start using a wheelchair at age 15. "The very thing I thought was going to limit me actually propelled me through doors I never thought possible," she says. In her chair, she could finally play sports: wheelchair soccer, football, waterskiing, basketball and then racing. Her training schedule—two to five hours a day—in Champaign, Illinois, is only part of what makes her hell on wheels: Her fiercest rival, Australian Louise Sauvage, who beat her at the Boston Marathon last year, nips at her tires in every race. Wherever she goes, Driscoll commands respect: "I've heard that the New York City Marathon doesn't treat [wheelchair] athletes well, so I don't race there. I'm an elite athlete. I compete where I'm treated fairly."

There are three ways to measure a champion: by what she wins, what she overcomes and what she gives back. Cynthia Cooper, the Houston Comets star, is that rare athlete whose talent is surpassed only by her humanity. It would be enough that Coop, as her teammates call her, has led the Comets to 71 victories and three WNBA championships in three years (she was named MVP all three seasons). Or that she was the league's leading scorer for the third time. But this is a 36-year-old woman who also selflessly girded her team while she was going through tumultuous times.

Last year, Cooper lost her mother to breast cancer and her best friend and teammate, point guard Kim Perrot, to lung cancer. [illegible] top of those

jean
the guts
driscoll